Scenarios III

Scenarios III

Stroszek

Nosferatu, Phantom of the Night

Where the Green Ants Dream

Cobra Verde

Werner Herzog

Translated by
Krishna Winston

University of Minnesota Press
Minneapolis | London

Published by the University of Minnesota Press
111 Third Avenue South, Suite 290
Minneapolis, MN 55401-2520
http://www.upress.umn.edu

Printed in the United States of America on acid-free paper

The University of Minnesota is an equal-opportunity educator and employer.

25 24 23 22 21 20 19   10 9 8 7 6 5 4 3 2 1

Library of Congress Cataloging-in-Publication Data
Herzog, Werner, author. | Winston, Krishna, translator.
Scenarios III : Stroszek ; Nosferatu, phantom of the night ; Where the green ants dream ;
    Cobra verde / Werner Herzog ; translated by Krishna Winston.
Other titles: Drehbücher III. English
Minneapolis : University of Minnesota Press, [2019] | Translation of: Drehbücher III.
Identifiers: LCCN 2019014736 (print) | ISBN 978-1-5179-0781-5 (pb)
Subjects: LCSH: Motion picture plays, German—Translations into English.
Classification: LCC PN1998.3.H477 A25 2019 (print) | DDC 791.43/75—dc23
LC record available at https://lccn.loc.gov/2019014736

Contents

Stroszek

Behold! I do not give lectures, or little charity:
When I give, I give myself.

—WALT WHITMAN

Preliminary Remarks

In the screenplay Bruno S. goes by *Stroszek* as long as his de-
personalized prison identity still clings to him. As the story moves
along, his first name comes more and more to the fore: *Bruno.*

The crucial feature of this story, also the hardest to describe,
is the constellation of characters. These characters should be allowed to evolve naturally—in a series of situations. When it comes
to Bruno S., the way he evolves will be easiest to predict: approximately as shown in Lutz Eisholz's documentary *Bruno the Black.*
We see him busking in courtyards, commenting on his own paintings, experiencing anger, distrust, and depression in succession.
This film is meant to create a monument to Bruno.

But Scheitz too has enormous potential; it would be a mistake
to label him insane. The French have a nice term for it, *para-
phrenic.* His contacts with the intelligence service; the mathematical studies with which he reinterprets the world and the
universe, demonstrating that Newton and Einstein were mere
dilettantes; his compositions: all are completely real to him, and
he can hold forth passionately on these things for hours on end.
During the shooting of the Kaspar Hauser film, he engaged in
the most uncanny dialogues with Bruno. Had they been filmed,

1

the result would have been a film unlike any the world has ever seen.

At any rate, the characters in the film should keep their actual names—at most with slight alterations—because their real identity plays such an important role. It's also important that Bruno usually doesn't say "I," referring to himself instead in the third person as "Bruno" or "Old Bruno."

As for the other characters, Eva will need a great capacity for reacting spontaneously, because we can never be sure what Bruno will do. But she's an actress who is up to the challenge. Then Driest and the Prince of Homburg: their faces say it all. Driest is already well known from *The Brutalization of Franz Blum* and the talk show with Romy Schneider. The public hasn't seen much of the Prince of Homburg lately; the most likely association would be that infamous interview on Second German Television's sports program in which he responded to every question, from beginning to end, with hostile silence. One sensed that if the interviewer had asked just one more question he would have killed him on the spot. The prince received a fairly long prison sentence after he forced a truck driver on the Autobahn to pull over when he wouldn't let him pass, then got out and beat the truck driver almost to death. His rap sheet includes such subsequent crimes as breaking into cars, giving false testimony, and, most recently, pimping. He's a tough customer, but he insists on having a part in the film.

Bud Donohue and Cholo the Indian are real people who work in Plainfield, Wisconsin. The United States has a number of places where something like a collective American nightmare can be felt physically: Wall Street, Las Vegas, San Quentin, Plainfield. The murders in Plainfield, a forgotten hole in the wall, have become famous in the annals of crime. Even if you go looking for the town, you can pass through it before you notice. At most you might describe it as an intersection of two roads that lead elsewhere.

Since knowledge of the actual people involved makes such a difference, an attempt will be made on the following pages to describe them in greater detail.

The film will have a November-ish feel to it.

CHARACTERS

STROSZEK	*Bruno S.*
EVA	*prostitute, vagrant*
SCHEITZ	*Stroszek's neighbor*
BURKHARD	*pimp*
PRINCE OF HOMBURG	*pimp*
BUD DONOHUE	*mechanic*
CHOLO	*his helper, an Indian*
BURHAN YÜCSEL	*prison inmate*
HOSS	*prisoner pending deportation (looks like Hoss from the* Bonanza *family)*
GOOD BOY BEO	*a type of starling from Borneo, almost as large as a jackdaw, his speech indistinguishable from a human's*

DESCRIPTION OF THE CHARACTERS

Bruno S.: he plays Stroszek. Short, stocky, scruffy. In lieu of a belt he uses a piece of string to hold up his pants. His fly is usually open, but he doesn't notice. Even in winter he goes without socks, his bare feet in loafers that look as though he fished them out of the trash. He has small, work-worn hands, the fingernails always black with dirt. You can tell from looking at him how often Bruno's been beaten, and it's also clear he has spent years behind bars. He has the look of an abused animal. But behind this exterior lurks a person of deep feeling, as you can tell when he paints or fools around on the piano. When he's talking to you, he sometimes grabs you by the middle finger and squeezes. He smokes a lot. It's hard to guess his age. His creativity has always been thwarted. While trying out colors for his paintings one time, he discovered that blue, yellow, and red, when turned fast on a disk, produce white. He'd like to publish this discovery. Bruno has a powerful aura; he projects a compelling, defiant sense of dignity. He has that rare quality: a glow from within.

Eva (Eva Mattes): she could resemble the character she portrayed in *Deer Crossing,* a role that suits her. She looks rather

"country," a bit plump but somehow graceful. Even when she says
"Fucky-fuck" to the Turks working on the construction site, she
doesn't lose her natural grace. She doesn't express herself well in
words, but she feels at ease with her body. Her taste in clothes
tends to make her look cheap. She thinks her English is good, but
most of what she says is gibberish. She has a powerful drive to
escape from the bondage in which she finds herself.

Scheitz: small, graceful, with unusually refined manners. Some
of his gestures express inimitable grandeur, for instance when he
greets someone. He stoops slightly, and with his skinny calves he
appears almost weightless. Delicate, waxy hands. He scrapes his
face raw every morning when he shaves. His eyes water constantly,
and now and then a tear rolls down his cheek. He speaks about
his theories with profound conviction but doesn't take it amiss
when a person responds with skepticism. He plays the piano very
well. Bruno and Scheitz treat each other with great respect. Only
on closer inspection do we realize that Scheitz is quite frail; the
impression of his inner lovability carries the day.

Burkhard (Burkhard Driest): big, strong, macho, exuding a
sense of barely contained rage. An odd combination of intelligence and brutality. He looks rather weather-beaten. Studying
law, robbing banks, spending time behind bars: all that has left
its mark on him.

The Prince of Homburg: a sinister fellow through and through.
Anything the most drastic spaghetti Westerns have dished up in
the way of villains pales by comparison with Homburg. He still
has panther-like moves from his time as a professional wrestler
and boxer. Thick wrists, powerful fists, stumpy fingers, a terrifying man, especially because he never speaks. Not one to be trifled
with, he looks incredibly rough and dangerous. His forearms are
covered with tattoos. His suits have a sinister elegance to them.

Bud Donohue: an auto mechanic, a skilled worker, gaunt, in
his forties. A narrow face with bushy sideburns. His skin has ab-
sorbed so much motor oil and grease that they've become part of
him. He never wears anything but mechanic's overalls. Extraordinarily glib, a phenomenal talker; he has a repertoire of sayings

that can make your head spin. Yet he's quick-witted in a lovable way. When he kicks the Indian, it's more histrionic than hostile, an expression of an odd comradeship.

Cholo: Bud Donohue's helper. A taciturn young Indian with a gentle expression. He has soft lips. Like many militant people of color in the United States, he wears a woolen watch cap pulled down over his ears. His most noticeable feature: he looks like a hunchback at first until you realize that he tucks his head in so far that seems to emerge from between his shoulder blades. Completely Americanized, good-natured, a show-offy gait. He holds his own against Bud quite effectively.

Prison, Four-Man Cell

Tight close-up: we see a beer bottle whose label has been painstakingly scraped off. As far as we can make out, the bottle sits on an ordinary windowsill. It's filled to the rim with water, with a withered silver thistle poking out of its neck.

From outside comes a faint sound of traffic, and suddenly we notice the reflection in the surface of the bottle: a straight road with little traffic, bent upward on the bottle like a rainbow. The cars appear to be driving across a bridge that arches steeply, their forms compressed and distorted, and as they descend they suddenly become minuscule, mere dots. And the same thing happens to people; on the upper arch of the curve they seem elongated, and a few steps farther on they shrink to dwarfs. Gradually heavy, melodramatic music sets in.

Above the bottle, above the street scene, which upon sustained observation appears melodramatic, the opening credits appear. We see the warped street for a long, long time. For an extended time nothing happens, and then something does: a car drives up the steep curve, develops an exaggeratedly high hump, and on descending contracts into a single dot. We hear the car's engine, and as the noise fades away we also hear sounds from inside the space. Someone is moving around, packing. Footsteps. A hand appears, picks up the bottle, and puts it down a few inches from its original position, and when we follow the hand holding the bottle, we glimpse heavy steel bars. "My TV," we hear Stroszek's voice saying, "you can have this, too."

The camera pulls back slowly. "A bit more," I say, and now we can see the entire space, a four-man jail cell. Two sets of bunk beds, and we immediately catch sight of three occupants. Stroszek is packing, taking his time. He gathers up a few toilet articles and stows them in a satchel. Hoss, a fat, good-natured fellow who is lying on one of the top bunks, reaches up and positions the bottle in such a way that he can see the reflection in the glass from where he's lying. We also realize that the window is so high up that even if you stood on tiptoe on one of the cell's two chairs you couldn't really see out.

On the wall by the head of Hoss's bunk several pictures cut out of magazines have been pinned up. They show the *Bonanza* family, and in the middle, the place of honor, is a photo of Hoss, with a genuine autograph scrawled across it, written with a thick felt-tipped pen. Otherwise only a few pinups from *Playboy* by the mirror over the sink. Burhan, a brooding young Middle Easterner, is sitting calmly on the toilet, staring into space.

"The thistle," Stroszek says, "has to stay. Herr Scheitz brought it back from the mountains. Leave it there, because the regs say you can have a vase but not a bottle."

From outside we hear footsteps, and a key turns in the lock. "I don't want to go," Stroszek says.

Prison, Property Room

A cheerless space, its shelves crowded with the personal property of all the inmates. Every object is sealed in a plastic bag and labeled with an inventory number. Two clerks check the admission list, and the younger man gets a form ready to be filled out in quintuplicate; he places four sheets of carbon paper between five copies of the form. The clerks have several aluminum pots stacked up on the radiator to keep their food warm. On the large counter, covered with greenish-black linoleum, the older clerk folds up a newspaper that was spread out there and opens a plastic bag that's already somewhat dulled. The other one checks things off on a list.

"Key ring," says the older one.

"Key ring, check," says the younger one.

"Handkerchief," says the older one.

"Check," says the younger one, checking it off.

Annoyed, the older clerk takes the grubby handkerchief and places it in a small basket labeled "Outgoing."

"Have you heard this one?" the younger man asks. "Two farmers are sitting on a bench in front of the farmhouse. One of them says to the other, 'Say, since when do your cows smoke?' The other one stares straight ahead for a while. 'My cows don't smoke.' So both of them stare straight ahead. 'Well,' says the first farmer, 'if that's true, your barn's on fire.'"

"Ha ha," the older clerk says. "Twenty-four marks in cash."

"Check, twenty-four marks," says the younger one.

"One signal horn," says the older clerk.

"Signal horn, check," says the younger one. "It plays a triad; he must have gotten it from railroad workers."

"Jackknife," says the older one.

"Check," replies the younger one.

"And here," says the older clerk, "an accordion, chromatic, a Hohner."

"Chromatic, Hohner," repeats the younger one, "and that does it."

Footsteps, knocks from outside the door; the older clerk presses a button, and we hear a sharp buzzer followed by a loud, ugly, metallic screeching as the door to the cell block slides open. We see a long corridor with multiple gates, the nearest one made of heavy steel mesh. Stroszek is shoved in from outside and trots into the property room, where he gazes around with lethargic interest. Feeling awkward, he makes a print with his sweaty hand on the wall, painted lime green in glossy oil up to about shoulder height, chalky white above.

The clerks grin cheerfully, then the older one assumes an official air again.

"Name," the clerk says.

Stroszek stands there at a loss for a moment; he doesn't know what's happening.

"Name," the clerk repeats.

"They've known that for two years," Stroszek replies. Did they forget to take their vitamins that morning?

"Bruno," the younger clerk intervenes, "you think we're joking when it comes to the regulations?"

"Stroszek," says Stroszek, "first name Bruno, one meter sixty-eight, oval, gray-green, none."

"Sign here," says the older one, "but not till you've checked whether everything's there."

"My signal horn, as per regulations. Shortly Bruno will sound a signal on it. Old Bruno," Stroszek says, "is about to gain his freedom."

The two clerks wish him luck and all the best and shake his hand. They ring the bell because the door to the cell block doesn't have a handle. It takes a while for a guard to come. To make the rather awkward wait less awkward, the older clerk assumes a paternal air. "Don't be in a hurry to get it on with women," he says. "Take it slow."

"Otherwise your ticker'll give out on you on your very first day."

Knocking is heard from outside, and the older clerk presses the buzzer, then hands Stroszek over to the guard.

The clerk calls after him that Stroszek should fetch the rest of his things from his cell now, then say his goodbyes, and the warden wants to see him before he goes.

Prison, Four-Man Cell

Burhan and Hoss are standing at attention, looking solemn. Burhan carefully hands Stroszek a piece of paper no bigger than a pea. As the camera focuses in on Stroszek's hand, we see that it's an unbelievably tiny paper boat, of the kind children make to float down a stream. Stroszek places the boat on a shelf where about a dozen such boats are lined up, each one smaller than the one before. "Yes, this is the smallest," Burhan says, and he's won; Bruno's and Hoss's fingers are just too clumsy to make one this small. Clearly the competition to make the smallest boat has been going on for weeks. In broken German, Burhan indicates that he worked with needles, scoring the paper, because otherwise it simply wouldn't have folded.

Now Hoss declares that he has to roll a bomb. Then we see what he means by that: he pulls a few loose strands and bits of fuzz from the worn edge of his woolen blanket, plucks at them till they're soft, and then rolls them into a tiny ball. He rolls the ball between his palms into a sausage-like shape about the length of his little finger, puts it on the floor, takes a small shelf from a book case after clearing it of magazines and books, and rolls the board back and forth under strong pressure. The shelf rolls faster and faster, compacting the wool into a hard object no thicker than a knitting needle. Hoss tosses the shelf aside and grabs the rolled bomb, which has now become hard and brittle, and breaks it in two. He blows hard on the inside of the broken surfaces, and we see the pieces begin to glow inside. When Hoss rubs a piece of paper on them, it bursts into flame.

Now he positions himself in the middle of the cell, legs splayed, and bends far forward. He holds the burning paper through his legs toward his buttocks. Hoss farts. The fart catches fire. That's Hoss's goodbye surprise.

Stroszek is moved. He weeps, silently, without any change in his facial expression. With deep emotion, and somewhat awkwardly, the three men hug each other. "I'm already gone," Stroszek says and goes. As he's leaving the cell, he gives a blast on his signal horn.

Prison, Warden's Office

Although the windows here also have bars, an attempt has clearly been made to simulate a perfectly ordinary director's office. Books, pictures on the walls, in one corner plaques from the prison athletic league, a handsome desk, but the door opens with the same screeching because it too has no handle.

Stroszek comes in, small, overvigilant, with that air of an abused animal that the prison, despite all its emphasis on neatness, hasn't been able to overcome. He has the accordion slung on his back by its strap, and in his hands he holds the satchel and a cardboard box tied with string. He doesn't put any of these objects down, even though the warden gestures to him to take a seat.

"Stroszek, this is your big moment," says the warden. "It's moments like these that make this work fun and enjoyable for me, in spite of everything."

Stroszek stands there with his luggage as if rooted to the spot. He doesn't know what to say. The warden emerges from behind his desk.

"Where do you plan to live?" the warden asks.

"At 5 Flottwellstrasse; Herr Scheitz kept my apartment for me," Stroszek replies. "He's my neighbor; he watched it for me."

"Still fond of the taste of beer?" the warden asks cautiously.

"You bet, Warden!"

The warden looks concerned. He flips through the files lying on his desk, looks up, then continues flipping.

"Bruno," the warden says, adopting a fraternal tone, "I have all your files here, and one thing's clear as day: there hasn't been a single time when alcohol wasn't involved. Not a single time. By now you have such a long rap sheet that I'm afraid the next time you'll get the book thrown at you, even though none of your convictions thus far has been for serious crimes. But one day a court will look at your record and conclude that you're a chronic recidivist, and off you'll go to preventive detention."

"Yes," Stroszek says, suddenly agitated, "that's what they want: to get rid of him. Out there the wolves are already circling. Yes, Old Bruno's the white black sheep."

"Let me finish," says the warden.

"That means," Stroszek continues agitatedly, "I can go straight to the bar and say to the waiter, 'Get me some white paint so the black sheep can color his face white.' Yes, that's how it is: away with him, they say, off with Old Bruno to the pen, we've got to get rid of him, make him disappear. Those are the invisible jails."

"Listen to me, Bruno," the warden replies, "there's just one thing I want: I want never to see you again. None of us in here wants to see you again, especially because next time you'll probably get PD. So Bruno, promise me just one thing: you won't touch another beer, you won't ever reach for a beer again. And also you'll stay away from bars, because that's where it always starts. Promise me that, cross your heart, and that'll make me feel better about letting you go."

"You have my Hungarian word of honor," Stroszek says, putting down his satchel for a moment and raising his hand.

A Street

It's late morning, and not much is going on. A little windy. An old man comes along on a bicycle, pedaling slowly into the wind. The effort exhausts him, and he goes slower and slower until he stops to get off and catch his breath, leaning against his bike. Now we see that he's so frail and drained that he probably won't be able to keep going much longer. Strapped to the luggage rack he has a frozen chicken from the supermarket, hard as a rock. He gasps for breath.

Very near him a loud electrical hum can be heard, and that awful metallic screeching with which we're already familiar. The old man starts in alarm. In the background a small steel gate set into a large steel door opens, and we see Stroszek trot out into the street.

In a few paces he reaches the curb and steps off into thin air, almost falling, like a person walking in the dark who doesn't realize that the ground before him drops off. As he stumbles, he grabs on to the old man, who's waiting for his spell of weakness to pass. For a moment both of them stagger before they right themselves.

"Excuse me," Stroszek says, "the hotel back there doesn't have any thresholds. Old Bruno has to get used to walking again."

The old man doesn't answer as he slowly pushes his bicycle along the curb.

A Street Closer to Downtown

With his luggage Stroszek trots along the street, looking apathetic. That's how a person looks when he's just been released. Only in the movies do children rush out of school yelling and jabbering.

A bar comes into view. Stroszek heads straight for the door.

Inside the Bar

The bar has the shabby appearance of the places often found near railroad stations: small and cramped, patronized by pensioners, derelicts, and pimps. A massive jukebox is supposed to lend the place an air of sophistication. On the counter a glass case with shelves on which stale sandwiches are slumbering. Behind the bar Frau Striebek, aging and sloppily fat; we can tell she's been through a lot. A scattering of jaded guests who've obviously been sitting there since early morning. An old man has fallen asleep with his head on the table; Frau Striebek lets him be.

We immediately notice Burkhard and the Prince of Homburg; they're sitting with a too-well-dressed younger man whom they've squeezed menacingly between them. Eva is standing nearby, looking rejected and superfluous. Some deal has just gone down, something ugly. Eva sobs; the men seem unmoved and don't so much as glance at her. She might as well not be there. Homburg looks especially brutal and frightening. He displays his violent disposition openly, while Burkhard seethes with suppressed rage. The third man tries to come across as innocent. The fancy silk suits over their bulging thigh muscles, their haircuts, and their behavior mark them unmistakably as pimps. Although Homburg and Burkhard are maintaining a quiet and amiable tone, we sense that some act of violence will occur at any moment.

"Oh, it's Bruno," says the woman behind the counter.

"I'll have a beer, Frau Striebek," Bruno replies. "And Eva, how are you, Eva?" Eva ignores Bruno. Bruno finds a seat at an unoccupied table. Now he registers the grim atmosphere at Burkhard and Homburg's table.

Closer to the table, Eva becomes hysterical; she sobs, pleading with Burkhard. We sense a kind of bondage. The men mutter under their breath, and we catch bits and pieces to the effect that the man between them was about to do something filthy and that he's apparently enticed a prostitute in some underhanded way to leave another pimp.

"Looka here, you can't do that, no way, not like that," Burkhard says, his tone exaggeratedly gentle and exaggeratedly friendly.

"We wouldn't want to start a fight here," Homburg adds, also sounding very friendly. "No need to fly off the handle. I say we stay friends, and you pass us fifteen under the table."

"Please, please, let me stay with you, I'll do whatever you say, just let me stay," Eva sobs. The men merely look annoyed.

"Did you hear something?" Burkhard asks. "Did someone say something?"

"I didn't hear a thing," Homburg replies. He glances under the table, where an elderly cocker spaniel is curled up, sound asleep.

From the words Eva is blubbering, we piece together that Burkhard has somehow pawned her off on Homburg, against Eva's will. But that seems to be a done deal and doesn't figure in the men's current discussion, which is focused on an entirely different transaction.

Out of sheer boredom Homburg flips beer on the dog under the table. The dog wakes up and trots behind the bar. Frau Striebek tells Homburg off; apparently she isn't intimidated by him.

"Can't you see how I'm crying?" Eva sobs, throwing her arms around Burkhard. He gazes straight ahead.

"People who cry a lot don't need to pee so much," Burkhard remarks. A sizable sum of money passes under the table from the third man to Homburg.

"Another beer, Frau Striebek," Bruno calls out. The proprietress brings Bruno a beer, and now we notice that she serves it without a glass; she knows Bruno drinks straight from the bottle.

Now our attention is drawn back to the pimps' table. Things have taken a dramatic turn. The violence the men couldn't let loose on the third man gets unloaded on Eva. Burkhard has stood up, his size terrifying, and Eva has promptly choked back her sobs. In a moment of terrible silence he looms over her. Suddenly his arm jerks back in a sort of electrical impulse. We see Eva go flying across the room. Not until she reaches Bruno's table can she stop herself. She falls onto a chair and remains there motionless.

Burkhard and the Prince of Homburg get up to leave. The prince prances a bit and jabs his left fist into the air incredibly fast against an invisible opponent.

"Guys," Homburg mutters, "put on your dancing shoes and get ready to face a southpaw." No one intervenes. With such incidents a daily occurrence, no one lifts a finger.

Eva and Bruno sit together for a while, neither of them stirring. Then Eva blows her nose, apparently shaking off what has just happened.

"Where've you been?" she asks.

"On vacation," Bruno replies, miming handcuffs. Silence. Eva straightens her clothes a bit. "What should I do now, where can I go?" she says, more to herself than to Bruno.

"You can crash at my place tonight," Bruno says. "Herr Scheitz kept my apartment. I'm making a fresh start today anyway."

Eva brightens up a little. "Exactly," says Eva, meaning herself.

Bruno's Apartment on Flottwellstrasse

An unusual apartment, where a glance tells us immediately that any semblance or concept of order is completely absent. There are messy apartments where one senses some kind of earlier order, but Bruno's apartment has the basic character of a dump where a few meaningful objects have been extracted and moved into the middle. Most noticeable in one of the two main rooms, which flow into each other, is the large, black grand piano standing in a sort of clearing; in the other room we make out an old-fashioned painter's easel and an architect's drawing board. All the doors are always open. On the opposite side of the unlit hallway we glimpse the kitchen, and behind it, on one side, a room hardly bigger than a closet. The apartment's windows are partially draped with old sheets and odds and ends of fabric, and the few places where we can see out offer a view of Berlin's most dreary neighborhood. The apartment is crammed with odds and ends rescued from trash cans and the bulky waste collection. These include some electric motors stripped from the devices they powered, a bellowing stag cut out of metal, coffee mills, magazines, clothing, several radios from the fifties, two of which are left on day and night, their dials illuminated but not so much as a hum to be heard. And musical instruments everywhere: several accordions, hopelessly beat up, a tuba, a xylophone on a small handcart, a gong. A television set that we can be sure, without even looking at it, doesn't work. Every spot within reach holds an ashtray; apparently they've never been emptied. Some of Bruno's paintings hang on the walls. Tubes of paint and sheets of music speak to the finer things in life.

Bruno is sitting at the piano, improvising. He looks happy, his eyes glowing. He utters a characteristic sound that in someone else might be interpreted as a laugh. He strikes the keys with heavy fingers, and every time he inhales he snuffs back his snot. Bruno plays with abandon.

In the dim, closet-sized room Eva clears off a couch for herself. She seems to be feeling better and tidies and arranges things, apparently undaunted by the mess; she must have seen worse. She moves like a person who's been set free, but on closer inspection we realize that she's trying to achieve a petty bourgeois image of neatness. She's beginning to exchange her bondage, her enslavement, for petty bourgeois respectability. She goes into the kitchen and pokes around until she finds some coffee. She puts the kettle on. She searches for food and comes upon hunks of bread that have been aging for at least a year. She tosses them into a pail, humming as she works.

At the piano Bruno has lapsed into a state of complete obliviousness. His playing lacks any recognizable rhythm because he fumbles for the notes and often hits the wrong ones. Eva brings him coffee on a tray with a little cloth that she spreads neatly on the piano. She's trying to conjure up some sense of a proper household. She treats Bruno solicitously and with obvious warmth, but preserving a bit of distance.

"I'll go pick up a few things and scrounge some money, then we can get by," Eva says.

"Aaah, the first cup of coffee," Bruno says, breathing in the aroma. "Old Bruno's got his freedom back. And all his friends waited for him. And this here, this is his best friend, his black friend."

He strokes the piano, running his hand tenderly over the keys. "And," Bruno adds, "there's just one thing I'm wondering about: what'll happen to his black friend here when Bruno's not around anymore? See, Bruno's going to die, and what'll happen to his friend—that I'd like to know. Someone's got to come up with an answer. Who's going to take care of Bruno's friend? Someday Bruno's going to die, and what'll become of his black friend?"

Entryway, Flottwellstrasse

The doorbell rings and Bruno opens the door. Out in the hall stands Scheitz, his expression festive. In one hand he's holding a cage with Good Beo, who hops from perch to perch, while in the other he holds a bottle of champagne. In spite of being loaded down, he manages to pull off an elegant bow.

"It's Herr Scheitz," Bruno says, overcome. He'd like to throw his arms around him but can't pull it off because of the cage. He begins to weep silently.

"Yes, indeed, it's Herr Scheitz," Bruno says.

"Beo," says Beo in the cage.

Bruno's Apartment, the Piano Room

Bruno, Eva, and Scheitz are sitting together, having coffee. They've talked themselves out. A cautious sense of something resembling happiness surrounds them. The coffee's been drunk, the cigarettes smoked. Now they sit in silence.

"Yes, Wisconsin," says Scheitz, picking up where he left off. "Who'd have thought I'd be going to America after all, in my old age. My nephew's sent me a plane ticket, but I'm going by boat. The planes nowadays are all defective."

"By boat," Eva says dreamily. "New York, Florida, and that park—what's it called?—where the bears roam around loose."

"The grizzlies," Bruno says.

"If Bruno had got out just three weeks later," Scheitz remarks, "I'd have been gone already, on the *Bremen*, in the middle of the Atlantic."

They fall silent again.

Behind Scheitz sits the old radio from the fifties, the green bands of its magic eye constantly blinking at each other, soundlessly.

Street in Berlin's Kreuzberg District

It's early on an autumnally chilly morning with hardly anyone stirring in the dreary area. Bruno, wearing several sweaters in layers, is pulling his xylophone on the little cart behind him. He has his accordion strapped to his back. He walks along quietly, a lost soul.

Rear Courtyard

In a desolate courtyard Bruno sings the ballad of the gypsy who leaves his homeland to try his luck far away. He accompanies himself on the accordion, and at the end of every verse he strikes a lingering tone on the xylophone. He has set up a music stand on which he props one of his own paintings on cardboard to illustrate each stanza. He has an appropriate illustration for each one.

People look down from windows around the courtyard. Quite a few of them are older women who apparently know Bruno. Children cluster around him, many with dark, curly hair like Persian lambs, speaking Turkish.

This scene represents an extraordinary event, and it's one of the core scenes in the film, hard to describe adequately.

Bruno performs the last verse with particular intensity, announcing it in advance. In general he improvises a good deal, commenting on the song and each situation it evokes.

From the windows the onlookers toss coins into the courtyard, wrapped in paper to keep them from rolling away.

A major, powerful sequence.

"Old Bruno," Bruno says, turning to the children, "has Eva staying with him now."

In the background, at the gateway leading into the courtyard, we now spy three somewhat older boys who take no notice of Bruno. One of them has pulled a plastic bag over his head and is huffing while the two others stand guard. He huffs glue until suddenly he staggers, falling forward. The two others rip the bag off his head. The boy stumbles diagonally across the courtyard; the other children show no surprise.

Bruno's Apartment

Scheitz and Eva in the piano room. The place looks a bit neater. A small bouquet on the piano. Scheitz takes his leave with exceptional courtesy, displaying a great sense of style.

"And Fräulein Eva," Scheitz says, "don't forget that the bird always needs plenty of water, and at night you have to cover his cage with a cloth."

After he leaves, Eva goes over to the cage, placed on a little stand by the window. The bird is full of spunk and in good spirits at the moment. He's blueish-black, almost as big as a jackdaw, quite compact, with lively, coal-black eyes. Beo in tight close-up, hopping from perch to perch. Then he suddenly inflates his throat and says, "Beo." Eva laughs.

"Gooood boy, Beo," says Beo, drawing out the *O*s. And then he begins to speak.

"Hello, young man," Beo says, "have you visited our flagship store already?"

He speaks without any trace of accent.

Eva pokes a slice of apple through the bars, and Beo pecks at her finger. Then he rings like a telephone. "Beo speaking," says Beo.

Bruno's Apartment, Night

Scheitz and Bruno in the piano room. Beo's cage is covered, and from outdoors lights and the sound of rain falling enter the room. The two radios in one corner glow but without any sound. The atmosphere in the room is tense.

Bruno lights one cigarette after the other.

"I'm sure she'll be back," Scheitz says. "After all, her things are still here."

Scheitz pages through an old magazine and comes upon a photo of an astronaut on the moon. A very odd dialogue ensues, becoming more and more a monologue by Scheitz. Bruno is a patient listener, but he can't completely hide his uneasiness. We also notice that Scheitz's devotion to him is due in no small part to Bruno's being such a good listener.

These moon landings, Scheitz maintains, are all staged photos that the entire human race has been taken in by.

"But," Bruno protests, "they showed the whole thing on TV."

No, Scheitz continues in a gentle, indulgent tone, that was all staged by Hollywood. A day on the moon doesn't have the same length as a day on earth; it lasts for fourteen days, followed by fourteen days of night. The moon heats up to as much as 302 degrees Fahrenheit, which one can protect oneself against for maybe one or two days, but after that the heat penetrates even the thickest insulation. It'll never be possible to conquer the universe with a rocket ship; people realized that back in the twenties, and as a very young man he conducted a study on the subject.

Should he ask Frau Striebek if she's seen her? Bruno asks.

Her place is closed now, Scheitz responds. But, he continues, he did his study with a space-travel machine, which he calls a space-travel machine on purpose, not a spaceship; he can't go into any detail. He didn't even apply for a patent, because all kinds of people were trying to steal it from him. But his contacts in the intelligence service proved very helpful, because the world just wasn't ready for certain things. The same was true of his completely new understanding of energy, and of atoms, which he began studying when he was only fourteen. Suddenly everything became clear to him. Newton and Einstein started from completely wrong premises: that he demonstrated years ago, nothing to it. Just think of the theory of colors.

"Yes," Bruno interjects, "with colors it's important to be very precise: *scientific!* Bruno paints his pictures very scientifically."

"Right," Scheitz chimes in, "just the fact that Newton uses the word *green* in his book on optics."

"Yes, green," Bruno says, "that goes well with ochre. Scientifically."

Newton had the temerity, Scheitz says, to use the word *green*, yes, *green*, despite the fact that the color green doesn't exist; it's a blend of the primary colors blue and yellow. The word *green* is sheer gall. It would be more proper to say that he came up with a new concept: *false gray,* that would be the right term. But the human race lets itself be hoodwinked, it's afraid of the atom bomb, even though it's easy to prove mathematically that no such thing can exist, either theoretically or in practice, because by definition the atom can't be split.

"But," Bruno objects, "they dropped a thing like that on what's-its-name, in Japan."

That, Scheitz explains patiently, was a fraud; it can't have been an atom bomb, and the pictures show clearly that it was carpet bombing.

Scheitz falls silent in midsentence and looks toward the door. We follow his gaze. The Prince of Homburg must have forced his way in without making a sound. The door is open, and he's leaning in the doorway, the very picture of menace. What makes him so frightening is his grim silence. Then a racket on the stairs, and we see Burkhard dragging Eva up the stairs by her hair with unspeakable brutality. She doesn't make a sound. Burkhard hurls Eva into the room. She looks as though she's been beaten mercilessly and one of her shoes is missing. She comes crashing in and still doesn't make so much as a peep. Burkhard and Homburg stand in the doorway in all their terribleness. Slowly and menacingly Homburg strolls into the room and glances around with casual interest. He languidly picks up Bruno's tuba. Then, as if upon reflection, he put his hand around its neck and slowly crushes it in his fist, the way one crushes a Coke can. With exaggerated slowness the two stroll out of the apartment, as if no one had seen them.

Bruno's Apartment, Day

The closet room half-darkened, with daylight shimmering outside. Eva is lying under a blanket on the pull-out couch. She's in rough shape. One side of her face is swollen, and her eyes are so sore from crying that she can barely open them. Lacerations on her forearms, bruises. Bruno has brought her tea and cookies, but she hasn't touched them.

"So what happened?" Bruno asks.

Eva shakes her head, refusing to say. We can see from her expression that she will never tell anyone what happened.

Street, Green Grocer's Shop

In a lively street with a number of small shops that display their wares in bins outside, Bruno buys a kilo of oranges. The shopkeeper treats Bruno very solicitously. Bruno notices that people are staring, watching him.

Now we see it, too: very close to him a flashy fast car has pulled up to the curb and has been standing there with its engine running the entire time. Inside sit Burkhard and Homburg, gazing with a bored expression at the fruit in the bin. They look right through Bruno and don't move a muscle.

Bruno's Apartment, Afternoon

Bruno in the painting room, working assiduously while talking to himself in partial sentences. He's chain-smoking.

"Green and ochre," Bruno says, "scientifically. This is the hell of banishment, and clouds like rocks."

He's painting a very odd landscape that has clouds moving across the sky like massive, lowering boulders. Again and again he breaks off and looks to see whether anyone's coming. We realize that Eva has disappeared again. Noise on the stairs, and Bruno tears open the door, but it's just an old woman in the stairwell carrying a pail.

Beo hops up and down without interruption. He hops and hops and hops. Time hangs heavy and seems unwilling to pass.

"I'm a bewitched prince," Beo says, "and you're the only one who can break the spell and save me."

Rear Courtyard

Bruno stands in a rear courtyard, singing a long, mournful ballad. People stare down at him from windows. As always, children cluster around him.

"Old Bruno," he says to a four-year-old girl, "is sad because his friend Eva is gone."

"And we're sad," the girl says, "because, because we have a star here."

"Yes," a little boy butts in, "it fell from the sky last night, and we can't get it back up." He shows Bruno a wooden star about the size of his palm, gilded, perhaps from an early Christmas display. Talking at once, the children explain that they tried all morning, and Willi is the best thrower, but they couldn't get it back in the sky.

"Well, give it here. Old Bruno will get it back where it belongs. Tonight he'll put it out on the windowsill, and it'll fly back on its own. But the night has to be clear for the star to find its way."

Bruno asks whether they've noticed a gap in the sky—they should check when night comes. He sticks the star in his pocket and leaves.

Streets near the Kurfürstendamm

Bruno wanders the streets aimlessly, like someone half-blind. A side street takes him onto the Kurfürstendamm. It's a mild, sunny fall day, and lots of people are out and about. The chic cafés are crowded with people idling the afternoon away. At one table Eva sits with Burkhard and Homburg. Bruno passes by, disappears, then suddenly reappears. Apparently it has taken him a few steps to register what his eyes have seen. Now he is highly agitated.

"Eva," Bruno asks her, "what are you doing here?"

"Hello, Bruno," Eva says indifferently, as if Bruno were only a casual acquaintance.

Something terrible is building inside Burkhard. Slowly and deliberately Homburg tightens the broad leather strap he wears on his left wrist. A waiter comes, and we see the familiar and preferential way he serves Homburg in particular. He senses that something bad is about to happen and quickly clears away all the glasses that have been at least partially emptied.

"There's a bad smell here," Burkhard remarks.

"Must be the dogs," Homburg says.

Burkhard glances lazily under the table. "No dogs here," Burkhard says.

"Well, they'll get here eventually, those dogs will."

Burkhard rises slowly from his chair and stretches portentously. Without waiting to see what happens, Bruno trots off like a blind man.

Bruno's Apartment

Scheitz is sitting somewhat alarmed but patiently on the piano stool while Bruno rushes around the room. Getting more and more hysterical, he finally bursts out, and Scheitz listens to him.

"It's all over with Bruno," Bruno says, "over and done with. Even back in '57 when I was in Tegel, my brother didn't want to come and see me. Bruno's the black sheep of the family, that's what they said. No place for him. But my brother, if I run into him, hmmm, you have any idea what'll happen?"

"No," Scheitz says hesitantly.

"Well, I'll kill him. And Eva and that other woman, they say Bruno has no right to exist, all he has a right to do is see the world in stripes, through bars. But out here the prison's invisible. First they take everything away from you, and then bam, you're gone. That's what I call the hell of banishment. Why did she go back to those two? She was so much better off here, but no, Bruno has no rights. So away with him, away with old Bruno."

Hospital, Interior

We back slowly down a long, long corridor, facing Bruno and Dr. Hoffmann as they amble along. The doctor is about fifty, fairly tall and heavy-set, but clearly with an alert, perceptive intelligence. We can tell he's made a point of taking time for Bruno. They must have talked at length already. Bruno seems calm and collected.

"Bruno," Dr. Hoffmann says, "you can speak with me anytime and come to see me, even at night if necessary. True, I'm here only on Mondays and Wednesdays. As you know, on the other days I'm at the prison."

They continue ambling along. They pass a bench where patients are waiting to go in for X-rays. A gurney carrying a patient who's just been operated on overtakes them.

"You know, Bruno, we'd be much better off in this world if we had an answer to the questions you're asking. I keep asking the same questions, and the only reason I continue to do this work is to have some assurance I exist. It's grotesque. Come along, I want to show you something."

The neonatal intensive care unit. Lying in glass-enclosed incubators are about a dozen children born at seven months or less. They're hooked up to machines with elaborate controls and to intravenous feeding tubes, all kept sterile. The children look like large grubs, and it's hard to believe that they're viable. Dr. Hoffmann and Bruno watch through an observation window in the next room as a young doctor and two nurses, all wearing masks, go about their work.

"We still have no idea who we really are," Dr. Hoffmann says. "Embryos go through a stage in their development where they have something like gills. And in order to see whether a baby is more or less normal, we do a very simple test. At seven months, babies have a highly developed simian grasping reflex, which has already largely disappeared in full-term babies. Take a look."

Through the window we see the nurses lift one of the little creatures out of the incubator and give it a thick, soft rope to hold on to, which they then raise in the air, a bit like a clothesline. The seven-month-old hangs on to the line and dangles from it. The baby opens its mouth and cries, but we can't hear any sound through the double pane. The child even grips the line with its feet, hanging on tight and crying silently.

"I have a hard time imagining that this child might become our federal chancellor someday," says Dr. Hoffmann. "Grotesque."

Bruno's Apartment

It's evening when Bruno gets home. Even out in the corridor he notices that something's awry. Scheitz is inside, and look, Eva, too! She's lying on her couch half-dead, in such bad shape that at first you might think she's been in an automobile accident. She's very quiet, very determined. She has injuries to her head and her arms, but apparently nothing is broken.

She speaks very softly. "Bruno," she says, "we've got to get out of here. I'm going to stay with you, I won't run away again."

"Should I call the police?" Scheitz asks.

"No," says Bruno, "don't."

"They'll be back," Eva says. "What can we do?"

"I have an idea," Scheitz says.

Bruno's Apartment, the Kitchen

Bruno, Eva, and Scheitz are crowded around the small kitchen table, which they've cleared off. Apparently several days have passed, for Eva is back on her feet. She still has bruises and looks battered, but she seems quite perky. They're bending over an old school atlas.

"Wisconsin, Wisconsin," Bruno says and licks his index finger to turn the page.

"Yes," Scheitz says proudly, "Plainfield, between Stevens Point and Wisconsin Rapids, that's where his garage is. On a truck route."

They leaf through the atlas, working out a plan. Scheitz is feverish with excitement.

"In '43 my sister married an Irishman. Donohue. And then they tried their luck over there. Their son's taken over the garage, and in the letter I just got from him he says he can always use help. The house has plenty of room for three, he says."

"But don't you think I'm too old?" Bruno says. "Look at my hair; pretty soon Bruno'll be as bald as a coot."

"Come on, Bruno, if we really want to make a fresh start, we can do it. Who says we have to stay there for good? If we don't like it, we can always come back here in a year or two," Eva says. "Just think: Chicago, New Orleans, California. Over there everyone gets rich."

Little by little Bruno catches the others' enthusiasm. He raises a few more objections about visas and money for the crossing. Certainly, Scheitz says, that'll take a week or two. And money for the crossing, Eva says, just wait—she'll scrape it together. For the first time Bruno begins to feel somewhat confident. He opens the window and takes the gilded star off the sill. "From now on," Bruno says, "Bruno's keeping it on him—so he won't forget."

Construction Site

A large construction site somewhere on the outskirts of Berlin. Major earthmoving. It's rained a lot, and the ground is churned up and muddy from the heavy trucks. Cement mixer, forms, a construction fence. On the steps of one of the construction trailers several Turks in rubber boots are playing cards.

Eva appears, teetering along in high-heeled boots and a dangerously short miniskirt. She's heavily made-up, her lipstick decidedly sluttish.

When she comes up to the workmen, who've been watching her from a long way off, she stops.

"Fucky-fuck," Eva says, not without charm, and smiles invitingly.

Bruno's Apartment, the Kitchen

Bruno, Eva, and Scheitz are sitting in the kitchen as before. The mood suggests the beginning of a new life. Eva seems most caught up in it, and she pulls Bruno along with her, but he too exudes something like hope. Eva counts out bills on the table; she's earned a lot. That should be enough to get them started, she says; they'll certainly be able to get by.

Scheitz solemnly unfolds a letter and bends over to read it. A Polaroid photo is enclosed.

"He writes, 'You can take over the house, which you see in the background in the photo, and Eva can work as a waitress at the truck stop.' I, myself," Scheitz says, "will be staying for only four or five weeks."

"This," Scheitz adds, "is my nephew, and the one beside him, that's his hired man."

Scheitz pushes the photo across the table. In the foreground, rather blurry, stand Bud Donohue and Cholo. They have their arms around each other's shoulders, and in the background we can make out a rather ramshackle farmhouse with a porch in front. We also see several cars up on blocks and auto parts strewn around.

New York, the West-Side Docks

The pier for ocean liners, bustling crowds. Cranes hoist luggage in huge nets out of the ships' holds and deposit it on the pier, the whole process conducted with colossal roughness. Some of the suitcases burst open or get battered beyond recognition. Chain-link fences sluice the passengers into the hall where customs and immigration formalities take place.

We discover Bruno, Eva, and Scheitz. Music by Sonny Terry accompanies the scene, giving it a dancelike atmosphere. The sounds die away. Eva looks somewhat more self-confident than Bruno. Apparently their luggage is missing, and Bruno begins to panic.

No hint of the excitement that used to attend immigrant ships' arrival in the New World. Many older people who like to travel in comfort, exchange students, tourists. Noticeable: the unconcealed threatening attitude of the police officers.

Scheitz is wearing a dark, old-fashioned suit in which he looks even more crooked than usual. He scurries around, and we're amazed to see how nimbly he moves among all the luggage.

New York, Streets

We see Bruno, Eva, and Scheitz on the streets of New York; no sounds, no voices, only the music continues. Bruno, as if in a daze, walks faster and faster. Eva has a hard time keeping up. The streets are somber, with tall, bleak brick buildings. Rusty fire escapes. In the background, off in the distance, colossal skyscrapers can be glimpsed through the gaps.

We see surprisingly many derelicts: people rummaging through trash cans, drunks, panhandlers.

Bruno has his signal horn with him; otherwise he has nothing in his hands. He toots on the horn, and the music swells.

United States: Landscapes

The music continues, pulling us along. An old Chrysler station wagon, packed to the gills. Eva is driving, and the landscape flits by. Bruno stares, fascinated, at everything; he can hardly keep up. Behind him in the way back we see suitcases, with his accordion on top. Just under the roof, crammed in, we recognize Beo's cage, but it's empty. On the back seat Scheitz is squeezed in among more suitcases. His eyes are watering.

The highway glides along. Huge tractor trailers zoom by.

The landscape takes on a life of its own. The Alleghenies dance, McKeesport with its smokestacks spins past, then come desolate stretches. Coal-burning power plants make the air in East Gary unbreathable. Chicago wobbles by on sixteen-lane highways.

We see Bruno's hand turning off the radio. The music suddenly breaks off, and we hear the car's engine.

"What kind of country is it," Bruno asks, "that confiscates Old Bruno's Beo?"

Plainfield, Wisconsin, Garage

Plainfield isn't a real town at all, more like the intersection of two highways. Three modern gas stations, a drive-in restaurant, a large parking lot for tractor trailers, always bustling, with truckers weary from driving all night hanging around, behaving in classic truck-driver fashion. One or two self-service stores, a somewhat older building that was once a hardware store, harvested cornfields, brackish ponds, a church like a Quonset hut, the cemetery nearby, a police station. The entire scene has an air of neglect, seems forgotten. The end of the line. But all around, so one senses, stretch the plains that reach halfway across the continent, unchanging, and there too is the end of the line. The farmhouses clustered at some distance around the intersection all have the same slovenly, barrack-like appearance, which suggests that no one means to stick around very long. Near the police station about a dozen mobile homes merely reinforce the impression that the people here are in transit to nowhere. All around towering masts for TV antennas, anchored with steel cables. A huge sky arches overhead, and the land beneath is bleak.

An electrical charge fills the air. Whenever two people touch each other, their hands crackle with sparks, and when a person opens a car door, he receives a mild shock; everything is charged; the birds are afraid to land on the trees.

Other than the restaurant there's no real gathering place for the community. What's missing carries more weight than what's there. It's a place without a history, without character, without distinguishing features.

At some distance past the town limits, down a dusty road, a junkyard extends far out into the fields. Only a few of the wrecks are piled on top of each other; otherwise they're scattered at large intervals. A messy, cavernous repair shop with a trailer next to it. Situated somewhat behind it is a sad-looking farmhouse, its paint peeling. Behind the farmhouse, a pond with ducks that waddle all around the house on the soggy ground. Several dogs. A hoist with an engine block suspended from it. Outside the garage several cars, fairly recent models, partially gutted.

Over the farmhouse door a garland has been hung. Outside we see Bruno, Scheitz, and Eva with Bud Donohue, being photographed by the Indian Cholo with a Polaroid camera. Bud wipes his hands on his overalls and strikes a classic pose, with one arm over Scheitz's shoulder, the other over Eva's. Cholo clicks the shutter, his chin pressed to his chest even more than usual. He's pulled his woolen cap over one ear at a rakish angle to show he's cool.

Laughter because the first picture turns out to be a complete blur. The difficulty of communicating with Bruno is treated as funny. Eva translates for him but misses most of what's been said. Scheitz's English sounds old-fashioned, and we can tell he learned it from turn-of-the-century grammar books and Shakespeare.

Now we see Bud grab Bruno by the shoulders, explaining effusively that he spent a year in Germany, at Ramstein Air Force Base in the Palatinate, and Heidelberg, and he learned one sentence that he can say perfectly. In German.

"Was ist los?" Bud says. "Der Hund ist los."

Bruno doesn't know what to do with his hands. Soon he frees himself and carries a few things from the Chrysler into the house.

Plainfield

Bud, Scheitz, Eva, and Bruno have all squeezed into the front seat of Bud's wrecker and are driving through Plainfield, headed for the truck stop. Bud stops at the intersection even though no car is coming from the other direction. He points out where various things are located. That way the road leads to Wisconsin Rapids, and that way are Oshkosh and Wausau, and an hour's drive north would take you to Winnemucca. He lets the Indian place names roll off his tongue.

The pickup drives into the truck stop, where two truckers are waiting for them. The driver's cabin of their truck has been tipped forward, the engine removed. Apparently Bud has repaired the engine block, which is now unloaded from the pickup. Bruno makes a special effort to be helpful.

On the way back Bud tells them about the town, becoming so loquacious that Eva more or less gives up on translating. Over there, Bud points out, is the hardware store where a trail of blood showed where the body had been dragged to the road; the woman who ran the store had disappeared. That morning someone had seen Ed Gein's car parked there, so the marshals wanted to question him. Not finding Ed at home, they peered into his kitchen, and there they saw her hanging, with a crossbar through the sinews of her ankles. She was already missing her head and had been eviscerated like a deer. The marshals then found a box with more than twenty embalmed noses in it, and Ed Gein's easy chair in the living room was upholstered with human skin. Later Ed Gein told them calmly that he'd gone to the hardware store with his gun and asked for bullets, and since he wanted an unusual caliber the woman had taken her time looking for them until she finally found two bullets. Ed had popped them in the barrel and fired them into her head.

And over there, Bud pointed out, was the cemetery, which had been closed for ten years already; that was where Ed dug around at night. And this over here was the farmhouse where Nancy Wolfe lived. The girl was epileptic, and one day she drove to the supermarket in Stevens Point and ran amok. She shot two housewives, wounded a cashier, and then she calmly stuck a head of lettuce in her pocketbook. After that she shot herself in the fruit-and-vegetable aisle.

Bud Donohue seems proud that here in Plainfield, over the past ten years, four of the two hundred fifty inhabitants turned into murderers, and maybe even five, since two years ago a farmer mounted his tractor one morning, one of those behemoths, and that was the last anyone saw of him. He disappeared as if the earth had swallowed him up, and the marshals searched for weeks, but he seemed to have dissolved into thin air. He, Bud, thinks the man must have been dumped in one of the local ponds; Bud has bought himself a metal detector and sometimes he goes out with it on weekends as a hobby.

Just in passing, as he pops a fresh stick of gum in his mouth, he remarks that he thinks his neighbor is a cannibal.

Inside the Farmhouse

Bruno and Eva inside the house. The rooms look better than we would guess from the outside. Clearly some new pieces of furniture have been acquired. In the kitchen a dishwasher hasn't been completely unpacked yet. A large color television stands in the living room. It's on, with the sound turned down.

Eva has made the place comfy, and we can tell that she wants to exchange her previous circumstances for petty bourgeois order. Tension can be felt between her and Bruno; a confrontation has apparently taken place that we haven't witnessed: there seem to be money problems.

"All the installment contracts," Bruno says, "are in Englandish, so who can say what's in them."

"Just stop, will you—I've heard enough," Eva says. "Here in America a person can earn money."

Scheitz enters through the open door, highly agitated. He's holding a small, very sensitive voltage meter, the kind used in a garage to test batteries.

He wants to show them something. From the first day he's suspected that so-called animal magnetism is present here in

measurable quantities. One can observe that simply and un-
scientifically from the fact that one gets a mild shock just from
shaking someone's hand. Since Franz Mesmer, he explains self-
importantly, people have been searching in vain for proof. With
one probe he touches the back of Bruno's hand and with the other
his own. An almost inaudible crackling is heard. From close up
we see the meter's hair-thin needle jump unmistakably.

Scheitz is very excited. Yes, way back in his youth he predicted
that this phenomenon would prove measurable.

Automobile Graveyard

On the edge of the sprawling junkyard, Bruno is working on a
half-gutted truck. Here the grass is waist-high in places, wilt-
ing in the autumn drought. He dismantles a gearbox assembly,
struggling because one of the bolts is rusted.

Near the truck is a harvested cornfield, which a farmer is
plowing. We see a second field parallel to the first, where another
farmer is plowing, and between the two fields a strip of overgrown
land about five meters wide. The farmers drive their tractors in
silence, seemingly impassive, cutting furrow after furrow into the
rich, heavy soil, turning when they reach the end of each furrow
and passing each other. Flocks of crows follow them, plunging
into the freshly turned soil behind them. The farmers plow closer
and closer to each other, and now we can also tell that they are
eyeing each other with suspicion. When they turn close to where
Bruno is working, we see that both of them have heavy rifles hanging from hooks on their tractors. When one farmer plows very
close to the edge of the overgrown strip, the other slows his tractor
almost to a crawl. The two drive past each other very slowly. The
crows caw raucously.

Garage

Bruno fishes around in a toolbox for a wrench but can't find the
right size. The shop is quite a mess, with pages from *Playboy* cal-
endars on the walls.

Bud Donohue is sitting on a wooden crate, carefully feeling for one of his incisors with a pair of pliers, and before our very eyes he yanks out the tooth. Beer! Bud yells and kicks Cholo dramatically in the backside when he doesn't react fast enough. Cholo fetches a can of beer from the vending machine in a corner of the garage, and Bud pops it open. This feels a thousand times better, he says, rinsing his mouth with beer. He spits out blood and beer. He holds out the tooth to Bruno with the pliers. He's glad to be rid of this son of a gun, he says.

On a high from this macho act, he begins to boast to Bruno about the broads over in Des Moines, Iowa, whom he describes as especially hot. He pulls out of his wallet a picture of a cheap-looking blonde wearing nothing but boots. Yep, that's how they are in Des Moines. Bruno more or less gets it and says, "Yes, Iowa."

Bud warns him to watch his back when he goes out to the truck because the two farmers on their tractors came very close to each other again this time. They've been feuding for years over the strip of land between their fields and have threatened each other in the past, and every time one of them decides to plow the other always gets out his plow too, to make sure his rival doesn't cut into the strip. If one of them ever plows a chunk out of the strip by mistake, bullets will fly, and if that happens he should get out of there as fast as he can.

When Bud sees that Bruno doesn't understand what he's saying, he sends Cholo to fetch Scheitz. The situation seems so important to him that he needs an interpreter. Bud leans forward and spits another mouthful of blood onto the ground.

Plainfield, Drive-in Restaurant

It's a typical drive-in, of the kind once found all over the United States. On this quiet Sunday morning the long-distance truckers are resting and taking time for a leisurely breakfast. Eva is serving them, together with another girl.

Eva has caught on fast and does a good job. The truckers tease the girls crudely, and Eva keeps her cool, having found how to handle the men, who obviously enjoy her company.

Plainfield, Swampy Area

Bud Donohue, Bruno, and Scheitz are poking around with the metal detector in an untouched, overgrown swampy area. Fallen tree trunks are rotting away, and pools, brush, and collapsed reeds alternate. It's a cold, misty November day. The three are in a Sunday-ish mood.

Bruno walks slowly, swinging the detector's arm back and forth. Bud is wearing the headset attached to the device, but there's also a small microphone that lets Bruno hear the humming and beeping from time to time. They stop and tug a piece of wire out of the ground.

On the bank of a pond the metal detector suddenly utters a sustained beep. The men dig excitedly with their hands and uncover a rusty plowshare. It's an old model, Bud informs them, at least fifty years old. He's pleased and excited because in his eyes the find's a real antique.

With an even more sensitive device, Scheitz says, one could certainly also detect the most minute changes in the earth's magnetic field. He once undertook a major study of changes in the magnetic field, proving that within the next twenty years the polar reversal would take place. That term means that the direction of the magnetic field will inevitably change so much that suddenly the magnetic South Pole will switch with the North Pole and vice versa. That will have unforeseen and fundamental consequences for all mankind, but his study was systematically suppressed by all the governments to which he sent it.

They continue on their way. Birds fly up in front of them, the swamp gurgles from its depths. The swamp is active.

Plainfield, Farmhouse, Living Room

Eva is sitting in front of the television set. She's in a bad mood. Bruno is helping Cholo repair a rotted window frame. We see that a tentative friendship is developing between the two men.

Cholo steps back two paces and gets a bead on the window, measuring with his eyes. Then he picks up a handsaw and saws a strip off a wide piece of molding. Bruno sees that the strip fits to a *T*. He tells Eva to ask Cholo whether he always works without a tape measure. Eva snaps that the two men should quit bothering her all the time.

But Cholo has clearly understood what Bruno wants to know and now takes a close look at the television set. He cuts a piece from a thin strip of molding and hands it to Bruno. Bruno holds it up to the TV, and in fact it's the exact width of the cabinet. Does he think she can see through him? Eva snarls at Bruno. Bruno is proud of Cholo, and Cholo is proud of himself.

Outside a car door slams, and someone knocks. A young man from the bank in Stevens Point comes in with his attaché case. He's very polite and very firm. He presents Eva with various documents, demanding missed installment payments. Finally he threatens them very politely with repossession. Eva translates only parts of what he says.

"Are things that bad?" Bruno asks. "Bruno's put in overtime." Eva saves the day by digging cash out of her purse. She has an unusual amount of cash on her, which surprises Bruno. He doesn't really get what's going on. The whole thing is over his head.

Plainfield, Farmhouse, Scheitz's Room

It's evening and all is still. Outside the window night has fallen. Scheitz is sitting at a small table lit by a standing lamp. He's writing something. He licks his ballpoint because the ink's not flowing properly.

Plainfield, Repair Shop

A rainy day, with clouds drifting across the great expanse of sky. The ducks are shivering as they scuffle around in the dirt. In front of the garage door Bruno's working on an engine; it's been hoisted by a pulley. He's taciturn, hardly looking up from his work. Bruno is withdrawing into himself.

Bud Donohue keeps up a constant patter, joking around. He's caught a frog and sticks his cigarette in its mouth. As if frozen with terror the frog sucks on the cigarette, inflating its body more and more menacingly. Bud says there are frogs that literally pop. He finds that hilarious. In the background the two farmers are plowing again.

Plainfield, Drive-in Restaurant

It's late afternoon, and only a few diners are at the counter. Music from the jukebox.

Bruno comes in, but Eva's not there. He asks rather awkwardly where she is. She's not there, says the girl who's pouring coffee, and she doesn't know where she went, no idea.

Plainfield, Parking Lot

Bruno wanders around the parking lot, which is crowded with big rigs. In one of the trucks the driver is lounging in the driver's compartment, his legs propped on the dashboard. He has the window on his side rolled down, and his left arm dangles out as he drinks beer from a can.

The driver waves Bruno over with a lazy gesture and points with his thumb to the sleeping cabin behind him. He makes an unmistakable gesture to indicate that fucking is going on in there. He lifts the curtain a bit, and Bruno sees Eva lying with the other driver. The driver in front says he'll have his turn later.

Bruno is speechless. He stands there utterly bewildered. Of course Eva has seen him. She pulls the curtain aside and snarls that he should beat it, this minute.

Bruno trots off.

"And just so you know," Eva calls after him, "I'm going to Vancouver with them. You heard me."

Plainfield, Farmhouse

Bruno's alone in the house. He sits there brooding. The television is on, but the picture has disappeared, leaving only stripes on the screen. Bruno just stares, making no effort to adjust the picture. He downs one beer after another.

Outside a car door bangs shut and a knock is heard. "Come on in," Bruno says in German. The man from the bank appears again and speaks to Bruno; he realizes that Bruno understands almost nothing, just stares into space. The man gives Bruno a document to sign.

"Give it here," Bruno says, "Old Bruno still knows how to write. That much he learned."

After the man leaves, Scheitz pokes his head in the door, looking troubled. We notice that his mere presence is comforting to Bruno. Scheitz sits down with him.

Bruno offers Scheitz a cigarette. "A live one for Herr Scheitz," Bruno says. Out of solidarity Scheitz smokes the cigarette, presumably his first ever. He coughs delicately from time to time.

Plainfield, Farmhouse

A crowd of about twenty people has gathered outside the house, where the entire contents of the house have been assembled. They stand around casually, feigning lack of interest. An auction is taking place, with the house and the furniture up for bid.

The auctioneer is a small, youngish man, his skin deathly pale and dark rings under his eyes. He's wearing a ten-gallon hat. In typical American auctioneer-style he talks so fast in a high-pitched singsong that it sounds like tape being played at three times the normal speed. The auctioneer points at each bidder, but even if we pay close attention we can't tell how the bidder and the auctioneer are communicating. The buyers nod so slightly that others can't see whether they're still bidding. It's a remarkable ritual.

Bruno stands there at a loss as his entire existence trickles away. He looks around for Bud, Eva, and Cholo, but aside from Scheitz no one's there who could help him. Bud and Cholo have made a dignified escape.

With a rap of his gavel the auctioneer confers each item on its purchaser; we recognize the man from the bank, who's collecting signatures on forms.

A spirit of something like resistance flares up in Scheitz. "Gentlemen," he says in German, "you can't do this to us. This is a conspiracy. I'm getting in touch immediately with my friends in the intelligence service, and then you'll see where things stand. You'll rue the day."

Stevens Point, Drugstore

Time has passed, and evening's coming on. Some of the stores have closed already, as has the bank. Bruno is driving the Chrysler, and Scheitz is sitting beside him with an expression of proud determination. He has a rifle clenched between his knees. Bruno seems apathetic. "This conspiracy will be nipped in the bud," Scheitz says.

They stop in front of the bank. With the gun at the ready, Scheitz strides on his skinny calves toward the entrance but finds it locked.

The drugstore next to the bank is still open. Scheitz heads inside, with Bruno stumbling along behind him as if blind. The only person inside is the pharmacist, a nondescript middle-aged man who at first backs away a few steps in alarm. Very cautiously, to show he's not reaching for a pistol, he pokes around in the pocket of his white lab coat for his glasses. This proves his salvation. "You're all in this together," Scheitz shouts and raises the gun. Bruno snatches the money out of the cash register, but it's only a few bank notes, small denominations. With half-hearted curiosity, Bruno begins to count, then loses track, and starts again. It comes to thirty-two dollars.

Like ordinary customers, the two walk out of the drugstore.

Stevens Point, Supermarket

Bruno and Scheitz leave the drugstore. Without missing a beat, Bruno keeps the money in his hand and walks into the supermarket next door. Scheitz stows the bothersome rifle in the car first, then follows him in.

Bruno shopping. It's a large, modern supermarket, with only a few evening customers inside. Calming music gurgles out of loudspeakers. Bruno pokes around in the freezer, looking for a turkey of the right size. He already has a bottle of champagne clamped under his arm.

Two aisles over Scheitz is pushing a shopping cart in which he has placed some fruit, and we also make out some canned delicacies. He strolls along, coming to the detergent aisle. Suddenly two marshals rush him from behind and tackle him. They have their Colts drawn. Before we can take in what's happening, Scheitz has been placed in handcuffs. "Aha," Scheitz says, "so you're in on it, too. May I ask who sent you?"

Only now does Bruno, who is trying to decipher the labels on cat food cans, realize what's happening. Completely composed, he walks out of the supermarket. Apparently the marshals have responded in such a hurry that they haven't heard the full story, and they don't chase him.

Plainfield, Garage

Bruno is fumbling around in the repair shop, talking to himself. We can't make out most of what he's saying, but this much emerges from his confused muttering: he wants to get back to Berlin. He's the only person in sight.

He takes a screwdriver to the coin box on the beer vending machine. All of a sudden the machine rumbles and spits out about twenty cans of beer in quick succession. Bruno downs one can in a gulp. He continues poking around. He finds bullets in a drawer and pockets two full boxes.

When he goes out to start the Chrysler, he's mislaid the key and can't find it. He takes the rifle and without a moment's hesitation climbs into Bud's wrecker. Then something occurs to him, and before he drives off he goes back into the shop to get the metal detector.

Plainfield, Truck Stop, and a Series of U.S. Landscapes

From a distance we see the parking lot, where only a few rigs are parked. Bruno drives the pickup slowly around an abandoned shopping cart, around and around. It's evening, and not another soul is in sight.

Bruno sets out, driving at a high speed. Landscapes whip by. We can tell he keeps heading in one direction; apparently he has a destination in mind. Like a wounded animal he drives on and on without stopping. He talks to himself. "Away, away from here," we hear him saying, "back to Berlin."

It's raining, it's November, dark and gloomy.

Cherokee Reservation

We're in the Shenandoah Valley. A road winds up the mountainside, with steep cliffs on either side, everything wreathed in mist. The trees have turned blazing red, the rocks have patches of damp moss, and the cliffs are festooned with poison ivy. We see Bud's pickup, which begins to sputter shortly before the last summit. With his remaining drops of gas Bruno reaches the top of the pass and lets the pickup roll down the other side without any engine drag.

We see a wide curve in the road, which has been broadened here to make room for a long parking lot and about ten little shops. At the switchback a drive-in restaurant. It's obvious at a glance that this place is a tourist trap on an Indian reservation. In the shops Indian women are selling hand-knitted items and woven blankets, and one displays tomahawks and spears. The whole place exudes hopelessness and bitterness. A number of men with fiery faces are standing around in full feather headdresses like in stupid Westerns, swinging their tomahawks and collecting a dollar from every tourist they allow to photograph them. We see a group of heavily made-up older women in Bermuda shorts and windbreakers enthusing over the scenery. Two Greyhound buses and a row of large sedans are parked by the restaurant.

Bruno rolls up slowly in Bud's pickup, the engine turned off. The truck stops and remains standing there for a bit before Bruno climbs out, his limbs stiff.

Cherokee Reservation, Restaurant

The restaurant is quite full, and we immediately see that a German tour group has made a stop here. We hear Swabian and Bavarian accents. The counters are crowded; the waitresses are Indian girls in squaw costumes.

We see Bruno squeezed in among several loud-talking younger men who obviously belong to a small-town sports club in Lower Bavaria. Bruno stares into space, drinking beer. Slowly but surely he's drinking himself into a stupor. Presumably he's poured out his heart to a robust, youngish Bavarian who looks like a butcher. The two of them down their drinks for a while in silence.

Apparently Bruno was hoping to join the tour group. "So you're traveling west, and there's no room on your bus," he says. "But at least Bruno's gotten to hear his own language one more time." More silence; the two men drink.

"So your old lady ditched you," the Bavarian says, his face flushed from the beer, "and they auctioned off your house. And that don't bother you one bit, right?"

"No, not at all," Bruno says. They toast each other. A squaw, chewing gum, pushes another beer across the counter to him.

Cherokee Reservation, Ski Lift

The sky darkens as dusk comes on. Damp, cold mist has settled over the mountains. We see a ski lift that's been idle all through the spring, summer, and fall; parts are rusting, and the chairs squeak as they rock gently in the autumn wind. We make out a dirt access road, a parking lot, and the lift station, which houses the machinery and also the pay booth.

Bruno comes walking through the mist, climbing the slope along the road to reach the lift station. He's talking to himself and seems to be drunk. "To the east," Bruno says, "Berlin's to the east, over the ocean." In one hand he's carrying the rifle, in the other the metal detector. Bruno reaches the lift station, and the metal detector beeps. Without hesitation Bruno smashes a window and scrambles into the empty building.

We see the building from the outside. Inside there's rumbling.

Light goes off and on, off and on. A sound of breaking glass. Suddenly a roar can be heard, the building shakes, and with much screeching and groaning the lift, motionless all year, begins to move. Pounding, shifting of levers, then silence. The lift is running, a ghostly sight, and the empty seats disappear up the mountainside into the cold, damp mist. Empty seats reappear as if from nowhere. Dense darkness settles over the slopes.

We hear a shot, which cracks so loudly that we jump. The lift keeps moving, on and on.

Cherokee Reservation, Ski Lift

Dawn, the day is breaking cold and damp. We see three police cars and an ambulance, all with their emergency lights flashing. It's a full-scale response.

We see marshals enter the building while others prowl around outside. Two men carry a stretcher into the base station but don't come out. The lift is running and running, a chilling, ghostly sight. In the building light goes off and on, and then we suddenly hear loudspeakers, mounted on the lift pylons for announcements. We hear the voices of the marshals. We hear levers being pulled, cursing. The voices echo harshly through the misty morning. The lift keeps running, unstoppable, meaningless. We gather that the marshals are trying to stop the lift, but they can't find the right lever. Obviously a dead man doesn't matter to them, only the lift. Curses, obscenities, as they shout instructions to each other. The lift keeps going.

The flashing lights on the cruisers, the cold, damp mist, the dark November morning. The lift goes on and on, on and on. The last thing we hear is cursing from the loudspeakers, dying away in the misty forest.

Nosferatu, Phantom of the Night

Wismar, Harker Residence

This is Lucy's kitten. More about her later. We will recognize her by her little black nose and white socks. The child who gave Lucy the kitten said she had run through flour at the bakery. So here is the little creature, clever and playful, using her paw to bat the small medallion hung from the window's crossbar. Outside the window lies the town of Wismar, and the medallion bears Lucy's portrait. We may call the man who painted the miniature image Herr Henning.

We do not need much time to acquaint ourselves with the house. At a glance we take in the bourgeois solidity of the decor; this world exemplifies the order characteristic of the Biedermeier period. Embroidered cloths under houseplants, comfortable furniture, gold rims on the porcelain. Still chewing, Jonathan pulls on his frock coat and removes the medallion from the crossbar. The kitten tries to bat it again as he slips it into his pocket. As he makes his way to the door, he takes a last quick gulp from his cup. Lucy goes to him and gently detains him, saying he knows it is not good for him always to eat in such a hurry; it worries her. Jonathan takes her in his arms; they kiss, saying their goodbyes, this time not in a hurry but prolonging the moment.

Wismar, Street outside Harker's House

Jonathan Harker steps out of his front door and onto the pavement. The small gabled house stands on the bank of a quiet canal, near the church. Outdoors the morning sparkles, a day in early summer. Pigeons flutter into the air. Lucy waves to him from the doorway and lingers there for a long time, pensive. Jonathan hastens along a side arm of the main canal, crosses a bridge, and disappears from view. Standing on the bridge with his back to us is a man dressed all in black, staring motionless into the quiet water below. His quiet, deep thoughts rock on the water's surface in the form of leaves.

Renfield's Office

An odd office, it resembles a dusty archive where, in the course of decades, Renfield has bizarrely become one with the files that no one ever reads. The shelves are filled to overflowing, as if pausing in the act of spewing out paper. Renfield, a smallish man in his middle years, whose head is propped up and supported by a leather neck cuff, sits hunched over on an overly high chair. His face expresses diabolical satisfaction. With a knowing air he is reading a missive unfolded before him on his desk.

Harker dashes in, hangs his frock coat on a hook, and heads for his work station. He shares it with another employee, a man crippled from the decades he has spent patiently bending over documents. Renfield has been waiting for Harker. He has an assignment he can entrust only to him, he says. Jonathan approaches him expectantly. Renfield assumes a confidential manner. Count Dracula has just sent him a letter from Transylvania, he says. He wants to buy a house here. That will of course necessitate a long journey. Where is Transylvania? Jonathan asks. Is it beyond the Carpathians? Yes, says Renfield, it will take time to get there and cost him much sweat, and perhaps even some blood. Renfield squirms at the thought, barely able to conceal his demented joy. Impulsively Jonathan seizes his hand; excitement has overcome the uneasiness with which he reacted at first. It would be good, he says, to get out of this town for a while, away from these canals that lead nowhere but back to themselves. He is ready to go.

Renfield slides off his chair and hobbles to a shelf. From there he hauls down an old atlas, so high up that he has to hop twice before he reaches it. When he plunks the atlas down on the table, it releases a cloud of dust. Renfield opens the folio and flips through it in feverish haste. When he locates Transylvania, he becomes ecstatic: Look! Look! Here it is, beyond the great forests! A dark and gloomy land, and they still have wolves there. He is not afraid, Jonathan remarks. The Count wishes to buy a handsome, old, abandoned house, Renfield says; perhaps the one down the street from Jonathan's would do. Renfield has gone over to the window. We follow his gaze and catch sight of a dark house, a partial ruin, with blank, empty windows, a sinister-looking place. Jonathan has his doubts. No, Renfield assures him, that is the one, that is what they will offer the Count; he, Jonathan, must set out this very day. Now Jonathan shows some surprise after all, but he allows himself to be infected by Renfield with thirst for action. Good, Jonathan says, right away, before the day is out.

Wismar, Harker Residence

Must it really be today? Lucy asks as she rises from her seat. She was sitting as in old photographs, pretty and composed, with the kitten on her lap, working on a piece of embroidery. Jonathan has stormed in, full of thirst for action, even neglecting to greet her properly. Now he puts his arm around her, because the news has indeed come out of the blue, and tries to cheer her up. But he does not strike quite the right note. In Transylvania, he tells her, there are still real wolves and real ghosts. A premonition of something bad creeps over Lucy; her face clouds over, and she says he should not go, he will be in danger. But a vague objection of this sort cannot shake Jonathan's joyful excitement. When Lucy tries to hold him, he gently frees himself and begins at once to pull open drawers and wardrobes. He packs his travel bag, hastening from room to room.

Lucy watches the goings-on helplessly. Her marital obligation to obey prevents her from interfering. As Jonathan stuffs two shirts into his longish travel bag, he exclaims, Wolves, bandits, ghosts—ha! Lucy shakes off her timidity; love gives her some rights, after all. No, she says, he must not go like this, she will not allow it. First she wants to go to the ocean with him, to the place where they would have most liked to have met. Jonathan pauses. Lucy, he says, I do not know—sometimes I am blind.

Beach near Wismar

A large, quiet beach with dunes behind it. The wind tugs at the clumps of seagrass. The ocean is gray, its large waves rolling evenly toward land. Above everything a great expanse of sky with white seabirds. Lucy and Jonathan stroll along calmly, looking small amid the vastness of nature. They are talking, but we cannot hear what they say; the wind carries their words away. The two hold each other gently.

Now the couple from close up. The sea wind blows through their hair and whips their clothing. It is a biting wind, but the two pay it no mind. Lucy stands still and looks somberly at Jonathan. She must say this, even if he will think it comes from the weak, defenseless heart of a woman. Jonathan has to urge her to continue speaking. In fact, this comes from the strength of her heart, Lucy says, an inner, nameless, deathly fear.

Wismar, in Front of Schrader's House

Jonathan is ready to depart. The horse is saddled. In front of the house belonging to his brother-in-law, Lucy, his sister Mina, and her husband, Schrader, have gathered. Mina is somewhat younger than Jonathan, a quiet, self-possessed woman, good-looking, secure in a solid bourgeois marriage. Lucy has pulled herself together. Jonathan kisses his sister, then he takes Schrader by the hands. He wants to leave Lucy in their care, he says; he is entrusting to them his most precious thing. Then he tears himself away from Lucy and forces himself to get moving.

In front of the house stand two mighty chestnut trees, laden with blossoms. The horse is waiting in their shade, held by a servant. Jonathan's travel bag has been strapped on firmly behind the saddle, and two leather saddlebags in addition. Jonathan is wearing a flowing coat that he has draped loosely over his shoulders and a large, floppy hat. He steps away from the family group, posed there as if in a tableau. When he is about to hoist himself onto his horse, Lucy, overcome with despair, tears herself away from the others and throws her arms around his neck as if trying to hold him back. Jonathan gives her another lingering kiss, but then gently and firmly frees himself from her grasp. Mina hurries over to support Lucy, who is about to faint. Jonathan digs his spurs into the horse's sides. As he trots away, he looks back over his shoulder and raises his arm to wave. We can see that he finds it very difficult to remain true to his decision and that it is costing him effort to appear manly.

He urges his horse into a gallop. Its hooves sound hollow clattering over the cobblestones. Along the canal vegetables and fish are being sold from barges; the movements of the buyers and sellers look frozen. Swallows swoop low, twittering. The horse's hooves send up showers of sparks. Crossing an idyllic bridge over the canal, Jonathan vanishes from sight. Then we see the city gate with its two pointed towers, shrouded in morning haze.

Lucy, Mina, and Schrader are left behind. The family group huddles together and remains in that posture for a long time.

In the Carpathians, a Wooded Area

The scene gradually goes from dark to light. We make out a dusty track through a mountainous wilderness. The heavy clouds of a summer storm loom over the peaks. In the foreground a massive bare tree that was struck by lightning. Behind it on the ground the bleached trunks of a number of trees downed in storms.

A weary horse plods along the trail, its rider likewise weary and dusty. From a distance we can already recognize him by his flowing coat and his hat. Jonathan lets the horse choose its own pace. A brook cascades over the path. The horse stops of its own accord and drinks thirstily. Jonathan slides stiffly out of the saddle, brushes the dust off his coat, and, with no regard for propriety, kneels and gulps down water, he too a thirsty animal. He fills his travel flask and rides onward, as weary as before.

Wide Sandy Beach near Wismar

The sea rolls and rolls landward. The waves wash far up on the beach. Lucy stands there in the wind, like Caspar David Friedrich's monk by the sea, gazing into the distance. She stands there a long time, motionless. In the background Schrader and Mina approach slowly. The scene gradually grows dark.

In the Carpathians, a Country Inn

It is raining. The hush of evening has settled over the scene. A quiet country inn that serves as a stagecoach station sits in a long, narrow valley. Bundles of dried corncobs hang outside along the wall. In the damp meadow facing the inn gypsies have set up an encampment. Covered wagons, emaciated scruffy horses, a camp-fire smoking from the dampness. The smoke does not want to rise; instead it drifts horizontally along the valley. Forbidding wooded mountains all around.

As Jonathan approaches on his weary horse, by now visibly limping, shouts are heard. The gypsies come running; they have never seen anyone like this. The barefoot women and children run toward him on the muddy path, and Jonathan dismounts. The gypsies cluster around him. The women touch him with frank curiosity, and the men too crowd around. The shouting grows so loud that the inn's door flies open and the innkeeper appears, his face twisted in annoyance. The innkeeper, a bulky man wearing a broad leather belt, takes in the rare, elegant guest at a glance and scolds the gypsies loudly. They fall silent for a moment, then resume their clamor. The innkeeper hurriedly makes two or three deep bows as he backs away, opening the door for the guest, and shouts at the gypsies once more in a strange, guttural language. He shows Jonathan into the house.

Taproom

A sooty rustic taproom with heavy peasant-style tables and benches. Evening is coming on, and lighted candles have already been placed on the tables. Strings of garlic hang on the walls. Stoneware jugs, strong wine, hearty bread, thick slices of bacon. About a dozen rural guests in their traditional garb. One table is occupied by taciturn gypsies with sparkling black eyes. At another table a peasant woman has a basket on the table in front of her from which the neck of a goose pokes out. The goose is trying to reach bread crumbs on the table. Quiet tippling, subdued conversations.

Jonathan is seated by himself at the only table spread with a clean linen cloth. His wine has already been placed before him. Behind Jonathan we can see into the kitchen, which is not walled off from the taproom. Next to the large stove we see, slightly raised on a platform, a bed with a thick eiderdown. At the stove the innkeeper's wife, an enormous red-cheeked woman, is busy cooking, her movements remarkably deft. Jonathan empties his mug at a gulp, wipes his mouth contentedly, lays his fist on the table, and calls for the innkeeper. Hurry up with the meal, he exclaims; he needs to get to Count Dracula's castle this evening.

Suddenly the entire room falls silent, as if someone had dropped dead. In the midst of the silence a crash is heard. Jonathan turns to look. In her consternation, the cook has dropped a stack of crockery. She stands there like a statue, her hand clapped to her mouth. One of the peasants chokes on the food he was chewing. The peasant woman with the goose crosses herself, and even the goose stops fidgeting and stares.

Jonathan realizes that something he said has caused this reaction, but he has no inkling what it was. Irritated, he looks around. On all sides he encounters expressions of disbelieving horror; the gypsies have turned to stone. The innkeeper is the first to regain his composure, and he hurries over to Jonathan's table. Does the young gentleman really need to go there? he asks. Yes, he does, why? Jonathan replies in all innocence. Does he know anything at all about his destination? Does he really want to plunge himself into disaster? Has he never heard that at midnight all the evil spirits there come out and wreak havoc? There are wolves with burning eyes, and people disappear without a trace, the innkeeper adds mysteriously. Jonathan dismisses these warnings as superstition; the fuss is getting on his nerves. But the innkeeper refuses to let himself be brushed off. He declares that Jonathan will not find a single coach to transport him this evening, and his horse surely needs to rest for a few days; it is worn out. When the innkeeper sees that nothing can dissuade his guest, he bends over and whispers to him that some of the gypsies at the table over there have already been on the other side, beyond the Borgo Pass, and they could tell him more.

The Gypsy Encampment by Night

The gypsies are sitting around a glowing fire, their eyes sparkling. Someone is speaking very softly. The rain has stopped. Among the gypsies huddled on the ground we make out Jonathan and the innkeeper; they have been using a section of a tree trunk to sit on. The circle is surrounded by pitch-black night. A horse can be heard stomping and snorting somewhere in the darkness.

A dark-skinned, wild-looking man with several silver teeth flashing in his mouth begins to speak. He has the voice of authority, and the rest of the circle immediately falls silent. He speaks a strange, lilting language, accompanying his words with graceful but unfamiliar gestures, while behind him stands an older gypsy in a floor-length sheepskin coat, breaking in every now and then to confirm or supplement what the man has said. Their tone and manner of speaking express a sort of finality.

The innkeeper leans toward Jonathan and translates for him. The young man should not go to the castle; the gypsy says there is a gorge on the way that crushes wayfarers to death; then comes a field of boulders that a mountain shook off its slopes out of sheer terror. He says that on the Borgo Pass the light parts a land that goes to heaven from one that falls to hell; never has anyone returned from there, never ever.

Once he notices that the innkeeper has finished translating, the gypsy continues speaking. His voice is clear and firm.

The gypsies also believe, the innkeeper translates, that the castle does not exist except in people's imagination. It is a ruin, he says, a ghost castle. Anyone who ventures too far into the land of phantoms is lost forever.

Bedchamber in the Tavern

A narrow chamber, with the raised bed positioned horizontally at the far end. Under the bed a stove is set into a stone platform, and wood is stacked nearby. It is already far into the night, and a flickering candle provides light. The room is furnished very simply, with a plain chair, a washstand with a large bowl and a pitcher of water, on the floor a bootjack. Under the bed we also see an earthenware chamber pot. Harker has draped his saddlebags over the back of the chair and is in the process of pulling off his boots when the door opens with a slight creak and the innkeeper's wife enters. She sprinkles a few drops of holy water on Jonathan and holds out a book to him, urging him to take it. At first Jonathan does not understand what the woman is saying in the lovely Eastern European language she speaks. Ah, he should read it, he realizes at last. Before the woman departs, she hangs a simple rosary with a small wooden cross around his neck. Jonathan resists a little at first, but the woman exudes such motherly sweetness that he gives in. The innkeeper's wife crosses herself and leaves the room.

Jonathan pages somewhat reluctantly through the book, which bears an alchemical symbol on its cover. He looks at the table of contents. Of vampires and human bloodsuckers, he reads. Also of shroud eaters. Of chomping in graves and revenants. Of the living dead who pursue the stranger through the village by night and leap on his back. Jonathan finds this all rather amusing and continues glancing through the book. He stops at one chapter: Transylvania. Nosferatu, the undead, he reads. The curse will rest on humankind, the curse of the vampire Nosferatu. He stows the book in one of the saddlebags and climbs into bed.

A strange roar makes itself heard outside. Jonathan, who had already crept under the eiderdown, sits up and peers out the window. He checks to make sure it is latched. But suddenly an inexplicable gust of wind extinguishes the candle. The room is completely dark except for the square of the window, through which the darkened moon shines. We hear Jonathan's voice speaking into the darkness, asking whether the wind can blow through closed windows now. From outside, like an answer, comes the bloodcurdling, long-drawn-out howling of wolves.

In the Carpathians, Valley, Night

Deep night has descended on the valley; darkness falls over the stubbornly silent forests. The moon rolls like a heavy wheel through murky clouds. In the background the few windows in the inn still lit look like eyes. Suddenly, very close by, the grisly howls of wolves, drawn-out, plaintive, wild. The moon slips behind a heavy cloud, and deep darkness prevails. Through the darkness we make out the green glow of the wolves' eyes. The eyes stare, and shadows withdraw timidly into the deeper darkness.

In the Carpathians, in Front of the Inn

The day has dawned bright and sunny, as if the terrors of the night never existed. A coach-and-four is drawn up in front of the tavern. Geese in the meadow, a scruffy dog on a chain. A few gypsies, keeping a respectful distance, crane their necks but do not dare to come closer. The coachman, a large, gruff fellow, is adjusting the horses' harness. Jonathan, carrying his luggage, approaches him and announces that he wants to be driven to the Borgo Pass. No road leads there, the coachman replies, and turns away. But Jonathan protests in astonishment, both of them standing on the road to the pass. He needs the coach, he says. He has no coach, the coachman says curtly and tightens a strap on the shaft. Jonathan sees that nothing can be done. He asks whether he could at least have one of the horses; he would pay twice the usual fee. He should take a good look, the coachman growls, patting the lead horse on the neck: these are no horses. All right, then, Jonathan replies, he will simply go on foot. He hoists his travel bag and the saddlebags onto his shoulder and turns to leave. The innkeeper's wife, standing in the doorway, crosses herself silently, and the gypsies gaze after him in silence. The coachman watches him grimly. None of this can deter Jonathan, who sets off, heading straight for the dramatic mountain range in the distance.

Road in the Carpathians

So there is Jonathan, striding along. The morning air is still fresh, and in the bright light before him rises a craggy mountainous landscape with snow-covered slopes and abysses, all glittering as if made of glass. One can see through glass mountains. Birds chirp their morning songs, and a clear brook flows toward Jonathan.

Gorge

The gloomy gorge appears bottomless, with a strip of sky far above exactly a fathom wide. From the cliffs on all sides tumble waterfalls, and the dark air is cold and clammy. In the depths of the gorge a terrifying torrent rages. The gorge is so narrow that in some places one could extend one's arm and touch the opposite side. A steep footpath has been carved into the precipitous slope. An abyss like this can crush people. The walls of the gorge are dark and damp. Mortal fear hovers over such gorges.

Jonathan quickens his pace, eager to get out of there, but he falters when he comes upon a terrifying waterfall that hurtles into the wild torrent at the bottom. Then he speeds along as fast as he can.

The Field of Boulders

We now see a steep slope on which Cyclopean boulders are strewn about. A broad, foaming brook rages toward us. The last patches of snow, looking half-dead and sullied, extend into the jumble of boulders, between them stretches of damp, flattened grass, like soaked diapers. We see Jonathan climbing the slope, a very small figure, at the mercy of the rocks. He toils up the hillside by the waterfall.

In the Carpathians, Borgo Pass, toward Evening

Here we are very high up. Nature offers no guidance. Piles of rock with bleached, tattered cloth pennants mark the top of the pass. Jonathan has paused to sit down. Jagged cliffs tower on both sides.

Large, cold, wet sheets of snow cover the mountainsides, above which the sun is setting heavily. Black and orange clouds flee one another like mortal enemies. An icy silence spreads over the scene.

Jonathan pulls himself together, and we sense immediately that he is crossing a divide here. Yes, and then too, the mountains are so high. Jonathan comes walking along, already a little below the top of the pass; he tries to project a devil-may-care attitude. He crosses a small stone bridge as if it were nothing. But we know: it is not nothing.

Rocky Road in the Mountains, Dusk

Now dusk is falling. Harker strides along. But what is this? In the last rays of the setting sun his shadow clings to his heels and becomes gigantic and distorted, like that of something nonhuman. The shadow grows grotesque, as if a monster were walking along. There's a whirring and whistling in the air. Something appears among the clouds, something enormous! Was that a bat drawing a gigantic zigzag across the sky? Since when are bats that large? As large as pterosaurs? And what is that? A shadow! A shadow whooshes silently over the mountain range, becomes larger in the valley, disappears, reappears. Harker stops in his tracks because he sees the entire landscape before him blanch. Then he hurries onward, his shadow still clinging to his heels. Far off the howling of wolves. There! Weren't those eyes he saw just now in the clouds? Why do the clouds seem to be racing? Forty days' worth of clouds in a single hour.

Now Jonathan stops after all. The sun has gone down. The day has gone into hiding, like a sick animal. Harker stands there. And already the night has closed in on him. Far ahead on the path a strange, wraithlike vehicle suddenly comes into view. Yes, it is a coach, a glass coach, of the sort sometimes used in funeral processions. It is drawn by four horses draped in black. The coach bounces along like a will-o'-the-wisp, a ghostly vehicle that moves without a sound. The horses snort sparks. Now the coach halts next to Harker. The coachman is wrapped in a dark coat whose collar covers half his face. He has pulled his hat far down over his forehead. Then the moon rolls into sight amid the clouds, and for a moment the coachman's eyes glow in the dark like those of an animal when one shines a light on it. He makes a gesture that brooks no contradiction, indicating that Harker should get in. Harker hesitates. Then he climbs aboard. He has no will left.

A jerk and the coach begins to move. A comet wavers past like a will-o'-the-wisp. Green eyes sparkle on the side of the road. Were those wolves? Because night has come, it is dark.

The Castle

High on a crag a ghostly, gloomy ruin pokes up into the dark sky. Crumbling walls, black window openings. Black clouds roll over it in the sky, and an odd whirring fills the air. Jagged remains of a tower point skyward like the fingers of a corpse that want to grab the sky. Now night covers everything, and the ruin vanishes into the darkness.

Count Dracula's Castle, Night

A gloomy moon shines on the silhouette of a gloomy castle. The coach drives through an arched doorway into a sort of forecourt. Harker climbs out, and the coachman indicates with an imperious gesture that he should mount the steps before him. Harker remains standing indecisively before a large, closed portal. As he is mustering the courage to knock, the leaves of the door creak, and slowly, very slowly they swing open of their own accord. Inside all is dark.

Out of the darkness emerges an almost rigid figure in a tight-fitting black jacket. Its shoulders hunch forward slightly, and its hands are cramped together. The legs appear to be long and thin, and the fingers seem to be long as well, pale, with elongated claw-like nails. The face is as pale as a corpse, the head completely bald. The ears are crumpled, and pointed like a bat's. The eyes that stare at Jonathan cause us, like him, to shudder. Count Dracula? Jonathan asks. Yes, he is Count Dracula, and he welcomes him to his castle. He has been expecting him and invites him to enter. The night is cold, and he must be tired and hungry, the Count says.

Dracula takes a lit candle from a ledge along the wall and lights the way. When he holds the candle in front of himself for a moment, Harker thinks he can see the light shining through his body. But that effect disappears almost at once, for the Count takes pains to keep the candle to one side of his body. The door creaks shut behind them.

Dracula's Castle, Dining Hall, Night

The dining hall, lit by candles. A fire flickers in the fireplace, casting crazy shadows on the walls and ceiling. The table, chairs, and other furniture very large. A long oak table and chairs with high, uncomfortable backs. We can tell how thick the walls are by the embrasures of the windows, which are barred. Despite its generous proportions, the room feels gloomy and inhospitable. Two trunks with iron fittings, apparently locked for centuries. On the table stands an iron candelabrum from the late Middle Ages, and indeed everything here seems to originate in that period. The table is set with a sumptuous meal, but for only one person.

Dracula takes the seat at the head of the table and places Harker beside him where the meal prepared for the guest has been laid out. Harker hesitates, not sure at first how to break the silence; out of embarrassment he begins to talk business, producing the papers on the house and a letter from Renfield. He explains that the folded sheet of paper contains the layout of the house, which will certainly be of interest to the Count. Dracula pays it no mind, however; he has his eye fixed on Jonathan. He should help himself, he says softly; unfortunately he will have to dine alone. It is almost midnight, and at this hour he, the Count, does not eat. Unfortunately, too, the servants are not available now, so Jonathan should allow him, the Count, to see to his comfort. Dracula speaks with exceptional courtesy, all in a very soft voice. Something about it conveys menace; his very presence fills us with trepidation.

Jonathan overcomes his nervousness and begins to eat heartily. The long journey has indeed made him hungry, and he applies himself enthusiastically to the wine. After a while he senses he is being watched intently and looks up. We see Dracula from close up. He is hiding his face behind Renfield's letter, which is encoded in almost illegible hieroglyphs. Slowly he raises his eyes from the page. His gaze meets Harker's. Both hold their breath for a moment, and then Harker resumes eating. Suddenly a small grandfather clock buzzes and begins to strike.

The clock close up. With every strike a little skeleton hits a small anvil with an ax. At the stroke of twelve a door opens, and the figure of death appears, holding a scythe. It swishes the scythe mechanically through the air, then disappears jerkily behind its door.

Dracula is highly aroused. He pricks up his ears. Suddenly the grisly howling of wolves can be heard from outside. Listen, Dracula says, those are the children of night. What music they make! He notices Harker's terror, but then Harker catches himself and assumes a sheep-like expression. Ah, young man, Dracula sighs, as a city dweller he, Jonathan, cannot place himself in the soul of a huntsman.

Harker has become shaky and does not pay proper attention as he cuts himself a piece of bread. The knife slips and slices into his thumb. In a flash Dracula is standing beside him, grasping his wrist. He is about to apply his mouth to the blood, but Harker's alarmed reaction causes him to pause. A terrible conflict takes place inside the Count. Then he releases Harker's hand, excusing himself with the argument that the knife might be contaminated and Harker could end up with blood poisoning. He should let him suck the wound—the oldest cure in the world. But Jonathan declines politely, saying it is nothing, a tiny cut like that is not worth mentioning. But to Dracula the wound proves irresistible; he can no longer control himself—or can he? No, he refuses to allow himself to show his true face so soon. He turns away, starting to return to his seat. But as he turns, his hand, as if no longer in his power, darts toward Harker's, and faster than the speed of light seizes it like a steel claw. The rest of Dracula's body spins as if electrified, and at that same moment his mouth attaches itself to Harker's thumb like a leech. For several seconds the two of them remain motionless, until the vampire lets go, as if struck by a blow. He recoils at his own loss of self-control. Jonathan should understand, he says, he wants only the best for him.

Harker, by now on his feet, backs away and falls into a large leather chair near the fire. The flitting shadows of the flames are joined by two large fluttering, flitting bats. Slowly, very slowly the vampire approaches. They should stay up together, he says softly; sunrise is still a long way off, and during the day he is always out and about. Overcome with nightmarish fear, Harker shrinks deep into the armchair.

Wismar, Schrader's House, Night

Lucy's room. She is tossing and turning, tormented by dark dreams, when a slight sound makes her sit up suddenly, her hair wild. She looks like someone who is not yet awake. The window is open, and the curtains stir slightly in the nocturnal breeze. A large black bat has become tangled in a curtain, where it is jerking its wings and clinging to the fabric with its hook-like claws. Its mouth gapes wide as it squeaks venomously. At the sound an abrupt, inexplicable shock courses through Lucy's body.

Dracula's Castle, Day

Harker, still in the heavy leather armchair, opens his eyes and looks around, drunk with sleep. Only with difficulty can he shake off the oppressive dreams he had during the night. What happened? Where is he? He looks around and recognizes the room, which only now, in the daylight, reveals its shabbiness. The heavy draperies are moth-eaten; there are spider webs in the corners, and dust is everywhere, as if the place has been unoccupied for decades. A ray of light enters through one of the windows, shining directly on Jonathan. Strange, hollow notes of a fiddle can be heard from outside, like someone practicing runs.

Harker yawns. His eye is drawn to his thumb, and he remembers cutting himself. He touches his neck. What is this? A mosquito bite? He gets up and goes over to a mirror on the wall. He sees two puncture wounds side by side, not large, not conspicuous, but certainly odd. For a moment Harker is taken aback, but then we can see that he rejects the thought that has occurred to him.

He inspects his surroundings more thoroughly. He sees that the table has been set, quite obviously for him. It veritably groans with dishes. Before he sits down to eat, however, Harker takes a closer look around. The main entrance is securely locked, but a door to one side of the dining hall is open. He wonders where his luggage might be; it is missing. The side door takes Jonathan into a strange, gloomy corridor, almost like a dark tunnel. From there a small door opens into a room with a bay window. Ah, there are Harker's travel bag and the saddlebags, neatly placed on a chair, along with his coat and hat. A bed, a candelabrum, a few pieces of furniture, all in manorial style. The bay window juts out like the prow of a ship, offering a view of a bright day and wooded mountains. Not a house, not a village in sight. A strange, unreal wind seems to blow through the castle, which seems like something in a dream. Harker pokes his head out the window, high above the ground. Far below yawns part of the inner courtyard. Down there in a niche he spies a ragged gypsy boy, practicing his fiddle with utmost concentration. Harker calls to him, but the boy is so engrossed that he does not hear him. An air of mystery surrounds the lad.

Next we see Harker stepping through a door into the courtyard, but now no one is there, although the fiddling can still be heard, clearly and unmistakably.

Harker continues exploring the castle. The gloomy corridor up above extends all around the castle, with other smallish rooms with bay windows opening off it. He comes upon an old kitchen, equipped with a stove but no other appurtenances. All the exits are locked up tight. Before Harker wends his way back to the dining hall, he opens a door into what turns out to be the library. A strange, gloomy, dusty space with barred windows. Bookshelves up to the ceiling, with thousands of volumes, left unread for decades. In a gallery reached by a short staircase a collection of stuffed birds and other animals. All these rigid objects placed without rhyme or reason. The passage of time has faded the collection to the point that none of the natural colors remain.

Harker returns to the dining hall and sits down calmly to eat. The fact that he cannot get out of the castle seems not to pre-occupy him. For now his bodily needs are well met. From outside the fiddling can be heard, disconcertingly hollow.

Dracula's Castle, Room with a Bay Window, Day

Jonathan is sitting at the window and staring out, deep in reverie. In his hand he holds the medallion with Lucy's portrait. He pauses and looks at it attentively. Then he extracts a notebook and writing instrument from of his saddlebag, reflects for a bit, and begins to write. His handwriting is fluid but full of character, and we can read along. Lucy, my dearest, he writes. There is no postal service here through which I might send word to you, so I shall keep a journal, in which I can record all my thoughts and feelings for you at home. So last night, after a toilsome journey, I reached my destination in Transylvania, the castle of Count Dracula.

He breaks off and looks out through the shattered panes of his window. Outside wind tosses the crowns of the large trees. Ravens screech. Jonathan resumes writing: I had oppressive dreams last night and hope that will pass. They have left me feeling torpid, but perhaps that also comes from the insect bites on my neck. Ah, well, I hope to bring my business with the Count to a happy conclusion this evening. The castle here is so unreal that some-times I am tempted to believe it is just a figment of my dreams.

Wismar, Schrader's House

We see Lucy at an angle from behind, as she leans on the window-sill perfectly calmly and gazes, lost in thought, at the quiet canal below. A tranquil image, collected and lovely, evocative of old paintings.

Dracula's Castle, Library, Night

Dracula and Harker at the large library table in the middle of the room. Candles provide the illumination. From the semi-darkness the stuffed animals stare down on the two figures. Dracula gets up and paces pensively back and forth. In stark contrast to the night before, he appears to be downcast. We are making the acquaintance of a vampire who is lonely and suffers from being a vampire. He says softly that he no longer cares for things like sunshine and glittering fountains that delight young folks. He loves darkness and shadows; they let him be alone with his thoughts. He comes, he says, from an ancient lineage. Time is an abyss, a thousand nights deep. The centuries come and go, and being unable to age is terrible. Death is not the worst; there are things much worse. He wonders whether Jonathan can imagine surviving for centuries and experiencing the same trivial happenings day after day?

Harker, baffled, looks up from the table and meets the vampire's gaze. At that Dracula realizes that he has said almost too much; he quickly changes the subject, and his tone becomes businesslike. He is pleased, the vampire says, that his guest has found such a large and old house for him. And did he not mention that it was located very close to his own? He would like to see the floor plan now.

Jonathan pulls the plans and documents out of his pocket; in so doing, he inadvertently drops the medallion with Lucy's portrait on the table. He tries to return it quickly to his pocket, but Dracula is quicker. Like the talons of a bird of prey his fingers seize Lucy's portrait, which we see from close up in his hand. Jonathan is at a loss; he holds out his hand, wants to offer some explanation. What a beautiful neck, the vampire exclaims before Jonathan can get a word out. That is his wife, Lucy, Jonathan says. A suspicion is beginning to form in his mind. He touches the vampire's hand to recover the medallion. Both of them recoil at the touch. Jonathan notices how cold the vampire's hand is. Dracula casts another greedy look at the small oval image, then relinquishes it. He places it on the table. The papers, the contract, he says, to distract Jonathan from what has just occurred: he wants to sign them immediately, on the spot. But, Jonathan remonstrates, they have not yet agreed on a price. He does not wish to discuss that, the vampire replies hastily; he will accept whatever Harker considers appropriate. His eyes take on a diabolical gleam; he has something in mind that he seems to be in a hurry to put into action. He asks how many days it took Harker to get to the castle from Wismar. Four weeks, Jonathan calculates quickly. Ah, good, Dracula says, by land, yes, that takes time.

Harker finds the whole situation uncanny. From the dining hall the grandfather clock strikes twelve. The candles begin to flicker. Instantly the Count's demeanor changes; his eyes take on an expression of rapture. Harker collects himself and bows curtly before withdrawing for the night.

Dracula's Castle, Room with a Bay Window, Night

A burning candle from close up. In its glow, the Lucy medallion. Now we see the entire room. Harker feels ill at ease. He slips out of his jacket and hangs it over the back of the chair. But then he decides not to undress further. A thought occurs to him. He fetches the book from his saddlebag, sits down on the bed, and begins to page through it. Chapter Two: Nosferatu, he begins to read. From the seed of Belial issued the vampire Nosferatu, who lives and nourishes himself from the blood of mankind and, unredeemed, makes his home in fearsome caves, graves, and sepulchers, filled with accursed earth from graveyards where the Black Death has brought in its harvest . . . the plague.

Jonathan puts the book aside and closes the door from inside. He opens the window and looks out. Close by, in the castle courtyard, wolves lift their heads and howl. Jonathan quickly shuts the window. He sits down on the bed and watches the door. Nothing stirs. Jonathan takes out the medallion and gazes at it briefly.

Corridor in the Castle, Night

A view down the gloomy corridor. At first deathly silence, then the howling of wolves in the distance. Nothing stirs, but there is a sense of something terrible in the offing. There! Did something move? From the impenetrable darkness the figure of Nosferatu emerges; now he no longer resembles a human being. His face has become completely rigid, and he moves along almost mechanically, unstoppably. Calamity comes on apace.

Room with a Bay Window, Night

Sitting on his bed, Harker pricks up his ears. What was that sound? Now all is still again. Then, suddenly, as if a gust of wind has gently rattled an unlocked door, his own door opens about a foot, creaking slightly. Then stillness returns.

Rigid with fear, Harker sits up straight and keeps his eye on the door. Now, as if moved by a ghostly hand, it slowly begins to swing open. Now it is wide open. Coming out of the darkness, the figure of Nosferatu appears. The figure slinks ineluctably forward. It pauses on the threshold, its gaze fixed on Harker. Slowly its arms rise over its head, like wings, like talons.

Wismar, Schrader's Residence, Night

It is a mild, moonlit night. Pale moonlight illuminates a room in which Lucy lies sleeping. Suddenly she is wide awake and sits bolt upright in bed. Her face looks as if she is still befuddled with sleep; in the depth of her dreams she has had a vision. A sensation of danger drives her out of bed, and she stands there bewildered, staring at the open window. In her long, flowing nightgown she looks as lovely as an angel. She begins to move, floating as somnambulists do, radiating a glow of beauty. The curtain stirs slightly.

Canal in Front of Schrader's House, Night

Schrader must have sensed something was amiss. He throws open the front door and dashes out onto the street, still in his dressing gown. He immediately spots Lucy sleepwalking along the very edge of the canal. The canal's waters are motionless and silent, and in the moonlight Lucy moves at an unusually slow pace, as if toward a destination. In an instant Schrader recognizes how dangerous her situation is. With quiet determination he hurries to her. When he reaches her, he speaks to her softly. Thrown off balance by hearing her name, she begins to fall, fortunately landing in Schrader's arms. He picks her up and carries her back into the house.

Schrader's Residence, Lucy's Room, Night

Schrader settles Lucy on her bed. At the door Mina has appeared in her nightgown and nightcap, holding a light. Call a doctor, quick! Schrader exclaims.

Dracula's Castle, Room with a Bay Window, Night

Like a terrified animal, Harker huddles on the far side of his bed. Nosferatu advances toward him. Drained of willpower and unable to move, Harker sees his terrible fate closing in. Very slowly the vampire bends over him, over his neck.

Wismar, Schrader's House, Night

The doctor has come and is standing at Lucy's bedside. Dr. Van Helsing is a dignified, learned gentleman, obviously rousted out of his own bed, for his shirt is not properly tucked into his trousers, and in his haste he has buttoned up his vest wrong. A housemaid was sent to fetch him, and now she is in the room, holding a bowl of water. Schrader and Mina hover nearby. Van Helsing takes Lucy's pulse. Lucy has fallen into a delirium and does not know where she is. Her gaze is unfocused. Like Harker, she creeps into the farthest corner of her bed. She babbles softly, making no sense. Then she suddenly cries out, Jonathan!

Dracula's Castle, Room with a Bay Window, Night

Jonathan is lying on the bed unconscious, his body completely rigid, his eyes half-open. Nosferatu is at his throat. Suddenly Nosferatu jerks back in alarm and listens. He has heard Lucy's call.

His face from close up. He listens, distracted. Some conflict stirs in him. His chops quiver; he is a creature only half-satiated. We can clearly make out two sharp, pointed incisors, almost like those of a poisonous snake or a rodent. Like a rodent he sniffs the air, registering something at a great distance. Nosferatu steps back from his victim. He will follow the call. Scrabbling like spiders, his hands leave Jonathan's body. He turns away and leaves the room, drawn by something far off.

Wismar, Schrader's House, Night

Lucy sinks back, calmer now. Her limbs succumb to a great weariness. Van Helsing releases her wrist and turns to Schrader, saying it is a sudden fever, her pulse rate is extremely elevated, she needs peace and quiet. They should call him again at once if she takes a turn for the worse. But he thinks it is nothing serious. Lucy falls into a deep, deathlike sleep.

In the Carpathians, Dracula's Castle, Day

From a distance we see the wild, jagged forms of the broken cliff in the morning haze. The sun rises above a wooded mountain and strikes the gloomy walls of the towering fortress in ruins. Sparrows swoop crazily around the massive battlements.

Dracula's Castle, Room with a Bay Window, Day

Harker is still huddled in his bed, in the same position as during the night. He opens his eyes and gradually comes to his senses. Now wide awake, he lies there for a while longer, his eyes open. Then, with a jolt, he leaps to his feet and pulls on his jacket. Now he knows beyond a doubt what goes on here. His movements express utmost determination. He leaves the room. The door is still partly open.

Dracula's Castle, Day

Filled with determination, Jonathan makes his way to the gloomy circular corridor. He throws open the doors to the other chambers with bay windows—nothing. Sun streams in the windows. A short spiral staircase, hallways full of nooks and crannies. Jonathan storms into the abandoned kitchen, pulls open the doors to the ovens. Nothing. With hasty, determined steps he searches the library, the zoological collection. Then the dining hall. Nothing. Now he has completed the entire circuit. He pauses for a moment to think, then tries the front door—locked. Without further ado, he seizes an iron poker from the fireplace and tries to pry open the massive door. But it is bolted too tightly—impossible to get it open. So the only hope is the courtyard. From there a flight of stairs leads down to the cellar. Jonathan throws open the door and hurries down the steps. He plunges into the deepening darkness. The only light comes from a flickering candle in a niche. Jonathan takes it.

In the gloom, the candle illuminates Jonathan's face as he walks down a long, vaulted subterranean passageway. Cold, damp walls. Another short flight of stairs. He finds himself in a large vaulted space. A coffin resembling a sarcophagus stands there on a stone platform. Jonathan approaches boldly and heaves open the heavy lid. There in the coffin lies Nosferatu as if dead, fully clothed. Motionless and pale he stares at Jonathan directly in the face. Horror grips Jonathan, driving him away. He turns tail and flees.

Dracula's Castle, the Room with a Bay Window, Evening

Harker has barricaded himself in the room with the bay window, blocking the door with his bed and the chair. He has armed himself. Somewhere in the castle he found a two-handed sword and a halberd hanging on a wall, and he also has the poker close at hand. Now Harker waits, determined to do whatever should prove necessary. Everything about his demeanor bespeaks courage and manly defiance. But at the same time we perceive signs of mental confusion; he is jittery, and now and then an odd expression comes over his face. A sound from below in the courtyard makes him start. He hurries to the window and looks down. What he sees terrifies him.

Castle Courtyard, Evening

The view from above. Four horses, draped in black, are hitched to a rustic wagon. In the wagon at least a dozen coffins are stacked to form a sort of pyramid. Nosferatu appears with yet another coffin, which he is dragging with difficulty. Evidently the coffin is filled with something heavy. Next to the wagon we see a pile of dirt and a spade, along with a grave marker in the shape of a cross that has been carelessly pulled out of the ground. The gypsy boy stands nearby, playing hollow-sounding runs on his fiddle.

Nosferatu leaps onto the wagon, opens the topmost coffin, which is half-filled with earth, climbs in, and closes the lid, and the four horses begin to move of their own accord. The little gypsy stays behind all by himself.

Dracula's Castle, Room with a Bay Window, Evening

Jonathan pulls his head in from the window. He seems to be thinking. A suspicion forms in his mind and becomes a certainty: Lucy is in danger and he must warn and rescue her. But how? He looks around. Without further hesitation, he grabs the sheet from his bed and pulls the frayed curtain from the window. Then he begins tearing both into strips.

Dracula's Castle, Exterior Wall, Evening

From a window fairly high up that overlooks the castle's exterior wall, Harker slides down the rope he has devised. Lumpy knots show where he has tied the strips together. The rope reaches almost to the ground. Harker descends rapidly. Suddenly the rope breaks, and he tumbles to the ground. He lands hard and lies there for a moment, knocked out. Then he tries to sit up. He has injured his shoulder and one leg. He slumps back.

As if risen from the earth, the gypsy boy suddenly appears at his side, a handsome, serious, delicate child, and gazes at him somberly. The boy stands there and plays his fiddle. It sounds like something from another world. Harker faints dead away.

River in the Carpathians, Day

A stormy day. A wide river flows briskly through a deep valley it has carved through the mountains. A raft floats sluggishly into view. Piled on it is the pyramid of coffins. Three boatmen in traditional Slovakian garb row the barge with slow, deliberate strokes of their oars. The motion has something menacing and unstoppable about it.

Slovakian Peasant House, Parlor

A simple room in a wooden peasant house. In the joints between the beams that are filled with plaster, pale blue decorative stripes make their way around the room. A masonry stove painted in the same manner, a low doorway, small windows, icons. By the stove, as motionless as statues, sit the farmer and his wife; she wears her kerchief low over her forehead. On the window seat sit four gypsies, preserving a grim silence, staring at the simple wooden bedstead before them. There lies Jonathan, ill and damp with fever. Next to him stand a nun and a doctor in a dark frock coat who has just examined Jonathan. The nun leans toward the doctor and whispers in his ear that woodsmen found the stranger unconscious in the forest. But it was the gypsies who brought him here, and she says she has her doubts about the story of how he was found. In any case, to judge by the condition of his clothes, he must have dragged himself a good distance over the moist forest floor. Not until he got here did he regain consciousness, but his mind is still jumbled; nothing he says makes any sense.

Jonathan manages to sit up a bit, and we see that his left shoulder is tightly bandaged. His cheeks are unshaven, his hair sticky with sweat and wildly unkempt. With his uninjured right arm he points straight ahead, as if seeing something. Mother Superior, he says to the nun, there are coffins, black coffins; the black coffins must be stopped. The doctor bends over him and pushes the feverish patient gently and firmly back onto the pillows. There he remains lying, utterly spent. The doctor and the nun exchange telling looks.

Varna, Harbor

A large, dark sailing ship, a schooner, is tied up at the pier. It is the *Contamana*. Among other cargo waiting to be loaded, we immediately make out the coffins. Most of them are piled on top of each other, but two or three are standing apart from the others. Much hustle and bustle. Dock workers drag heavy sacks over a swaying gangplank onto the ship. They are all barefoot.

Customs officials have gathered near the coffins, along with the captain of the *Contamana* and several sailors. The customs inspector circles one of the coffins, hesitates, then circles it again. Strange, he comments, the papers all seemed to be in order. The captain, a man in his middle years who radiates manly sagacity and a lifetime of solid experience, examines his own set of papers. From Varna to Wismar, he reads. The contents are declared as garden soil for botanical experiments. The inspector directs him to open one of the containers; he wants to see for himself. Dock workers pull one of the coffins out of the stack and pry open the lid with crowbars. In fact, only dirt. Dump it out, the inspector orders. The workers tip the coffin and shake its entire contents onto the ground. When they lift the coffin away, about twenty rats crawl out. A rat creeps over the bare foot of one of the workers. Disgusted, he pushes it away. As he does so, the rat apparently bites him. The worker curses and grabs his foot, where we see a clean little bite mark.

Wismar, Insane Asylum, Office of the Director

Dr. Van Helsing is working on papers in his office. The room is generously sized, and it appears to be equipped for medical research. On his desk Van Helsing has a microscope, a number of test tubes, and tissue samples. The shelves are packed with thick medical tomes. Anatomical drawings hang on the walls, prominent among them drawings of parts of the human brain. In a jar of formaldehyde a newborn in the fetal position with a deformed, abnormally large head.

An attendant bursts in without knocking, out of breath and frightened. The patient admitted to the closed ward yesterday is having an attack. Van Helsing breaks off his work at once and follows the attendant out of the room.

Insane Asylum, Cell

Van Helsing and the attendant enter the narrow cell, furnished with nothing but a wooden cot. The window, high up in the wall, has multiple sets of bars. The patient on the cot is cowering like an animal. He has covered his head and is sucking or eating something. He pays no attention to the men as they enter. Then, suddenly he jumps out of bed, and we see that it is Renfield, who has gone completely mad. His face twitches. He hops up and down like a goblin. At the window he snags a fly with a jerky gesture and immediately begins to suck it. Blood is life! he exclaims several times. The attendant asks him what he has there and orders him to hand it over. He then takes the fly away from him. Renfield is thunderstruck. His twisted face falls apart. He screams and cries like a two-year-old and wets his pants. Standing in a puddle of urine, Renfield begins to bawl.

Van Helsing asks whether this has happened before. Yes, the attendant replies, instead of meals he asks for flies. When the two men take their eyes off the patient for a moment, Renfield jumps the attendant and tries to get at his neck. A struggle ensues. From the corridor two more attendants rush in and force Renfield into a straitjacket. Renfield bawls and rolls from side to side. Then, all of a sudden he falls silent. Hush, he says, he hears sails rustling.

Open Sea, the *Contamana,* Day

Out on the ocean, with no land in sight, gray, powerful waves and a gray, rainy sky above. The *Contamana* travels from right to left, her sails billowing as she pitches in the stormy sea.

Wismar, in the Dunes, Day

Lucy is sitting on a bench in the dunes. The day is gray, the wind gusty. The gray, stormy sea rolls slowly and ceaselessly shoreward. Gulls are blown hither and thither by the wind. Stuck into the sand are several cross-shaped grave markers leaning at odd angles, half-buried by time and storms. Lucy sits there for a long time, gazing out to sea.

Mina and Schrader come trudging through the sand. Schrader is holding on to his hat to keep it from being blown from his head. They stop in front of Lucy. Lucy looks at them quizzically. Still no letter, Schrader says, but she should not worry; the mails in Transylvania are so unreliable. The postal courier says so himself. But Lucy can no longer be mollified. Something must have happened to Jonathan, she says, she is certain. Mina comes closer and places her hand reassuringly on Lucy's shoulder, saying Lucy can be sure the Lord hears her prayers. The Lord, Lucy replies, is so far from people in their hour of need.

Slovakian Peasant House, Parlor

Harker's sickroom is in an uproar, the gypsies especially troubled, because standing among them, his legs shaky and his eyes glassy, is Harker, struggling into his coat. The oldest gypsy tries to hold him back, speaking to him with obvious concern in his foreign tongue. The mother superior is also present. She tries to push him gently back toward the bed. The young man is still too ill to travel, she says. The coffins, Jonathan mumbles, he must reach Wismar before the coffins. The nun interrupts him, urging the young man at least to wait until the next day, when the doctor will come again. No, Jonathan protests, Lucy is in danger, he must save her. The feverish man refuses to be deterred. He pays no heed to the pain in his shoulder, over which he can barely pull his coat. The coffins, he says, a dreadful misfortune is on its way.

The *Contamana,* Captain's Cabin, Day

The captain at the map table. Nautical maps, various instruments and measuring devices. With a heavy, clumsy hand the captain is entering notes in the ship's log. The cabin rolls and pitches. We read the entry: "A curse seems to have been hovering over the ship ever since we left the Black Sea. One after another four sailors and a mate have fallen ill and died. One sailor and the cook have vanished without a trace. A rumor sprang up and frightened the men, to the effect that a stranger has stowed away on board, but we have searched everywhere. The rats are a real plague, however. We continue to try to hold a northwesterly course. Wind steady, 12 knots."

Wismar, Insane Asylum, Renfield's Cell

Lucy, accompanied by Van Helsing and an attendant, is in Renfield's cell. He cowers on his cot, unresponsive, his eyes fixed on the flies buzzing around the window. In the meantime the straitjacket has been removed. There are certainly times, Van Helsing says, when one can hold a rational discussion with the patient, but he must warn her not to expect too much. Lucy seems determined, however, to do her utmost. Taking heart, she moves close to Renfield, who does not look at her. Herr Renfield, she begins, was it not he who commissioned her husband to go to Transylvania? For weeks now she has had no word from him, and she is very worried. She wants to go and find him. She should not do that, Renfield says suddenly, she should wait; the Master is coming. Whom does he mean? Van Helsing asks; he should explain. The lord of the rats, Renfield says; the army is hungry, and four hundred thousand strong.

Then Renfield begins to laugh, a screeching, horrendous laughter with which he assaults the visitors to his cell. Van Helsing takes Lucy by the shoulder and hurries her away, explaining that the patient suffers from a mental aberration, and it would be best to leave. Only the attendant stays behind, beginning to sweep the floor of the cell.

Suddenly Renfield's attention fixes on a neatly folded newspaper poking out of a pocket in the attendant's jacket. When the attendant, intent on his sweeping, comes close to Renfield with his back to him, Renfield takes two steps on tiptoes and surreptitiously extracts the paper from the attendant's pocket. Renfield quickly stuffs the paper under his blanket and pretends to hunt for flies in the window. Taking his broom, the attendant leaves the cell. We hear the key turning in the lock.

Renfield immediately begins to comb through the paper. He has something specific in mind. There: he has found it. Among the news briefs we read along with him: "Plague. In Transylvania and the Black Sea port of Varna an outbreak of the plague has occurred, and the epidemic is spreading rapidly. Young women in particular have fallen prey to it. All the victims have odd bite marks on their necks, the source of which still mystifies doctors. Entire regions have been decimated. Cattle have experienced epileptic seizures, then expired." Renfield looks up from the paper and sniffs the air. His expression is knowing; slowly laughter wells up in him. It is grisly, this laughter.

In the Carpathians, Countryside, Day

A mountainous area in which one can see for a great distance. It is a very wild, lonely landscape. A dusty road. Harker appears on horseback, riding from right to left. He is so ill that he can barely stay on the horse. Nonetheless he feels driven to make haste. His gaze is demented with fever, his hair blowing in the wind.

Open Sea, Dusk

We see the *Contamana*, likewise moving from right to left. We can make out no crew on board, at least not at this distance. The ship forges briskly through the waves.

A large bat accompanies the ship. Then, with slow, majestic wingbeats it settles onto the ship.

The *Contamana,* Quarterdeck, Evening

The captain is the only man left on board. Manfully he stands at the helm. Come what may, he will not abandon this post. He seizes a rope and without hesitation lashes himself to the helm. He looks exhausted, but his expression is solemn and determined; he stands there defiantly. The sun has set.

The hatch, seen from the cargo bay. Black and unbending, Nosferatu's silhouette appears against the dimming sky. He approaches, slowly, inexorably, his claws extended. His chops quiver slightly. Sails whip in the wind.

On the deck of the *Contamana*. We move toward the captain. His torso rears back, his arm stretches out to ward off the danger, but his legs remain firmly in place.

Open Sea, Nightfall

Darkness has settled over the ocean. In the last faint light we see the black outlines of the *Contamana* as it forges ahead. The death ship's wake still foams white.

Wismar, Schrader's Residence, Day

It is a quiet afternoon, and a holiday stillness fills the house. Lucy is dressed for a journey, in hat and coat. She seems uneasy. Mina is with her, sitting quietly near the window with her embroidery hoop. Somewhere in the house a clock strikes four, and promptly a grandfather clock in the next room answers softly with four strikes. Mina should listen, Lucy says, to the way the clocks in the dark house call out to each other. But, Mina protests, the sky is still bright. No, Lucy replies; if she wanted to judge by the darkness that always surrounds her, she would have to believe that the sun has gone down forever. The world has become bleak and empty; she keeps seeing a bleak coast before her and has no idea what that means.

Along the Coast

A gloomy sea washes up on a bleak land that repeatedly vanishes in churning fog. Wild, uninhabited mountains rear up, visible only briefly, everything flickering, gray on gray. And another coastline, even rougher. Here the clouds are enormous. And onto the bare, battered shore protrude ships' skeletons. Their covering chewed away, the ribs of these rumps stare into the stormy air. Wreck lies next to wreck, as if all the ships in the world have sunk, one after the other. The scene goes dark.

Wismar, Harbor, Daybreak

The harbor lies quietly in the morning haze. Work has not yet started. Silently the *Contamana* glides into port with no crew at all, a ghost ship. Very calmly the ship maneuvers herself alongside the pier. We hear a soft scraping sound, and then the ship comes to a standstill. Nothing moves. There she lies.

Wismar, Insane Asylum, Renfield's Cell, Day

Under his blanket Renfield has curled up in a ball. He lies there, listening. Then he sits up and sniffs the air. He seizes hold of the grille over his window, hoists himself up, and looks out. Demented laughter shakes his entire body. The Master is here, yes, the Master is here, he chortles, ecstatic with certainty.

A Road, Day

An open field with large clouds floating overhead, an enormous horizon. The countryside is flatter here, crisscrossed by canals. Barges lie at anchor. The vanes of windmills turn sedately. Down a long road a rider gallops from right to left, not sparing his horse, overheated and foaming at the mouth. We recognize Jonathan Harker, barely managing to stay in his saddle. His coat flaps around him.

Wismar, Harbor, Day

At the spot where the *Contamana* has docked herself, twenty or thirty people have gathered. Townsfolk filled with curiosity, a few children, barefoot dockworkers, dignified gentlemen from the customs office and the harbor agency, the town council. The harbormaster turns to one of the workers and instructs him to lay a plank; the ship must be inspected. The worker does as he is told, and the harbormaster goes on board, followed by the gentlemen from the customs office.

Contamana, Deck

The first thing they come upon is the captain, dead, but still held by the rope with which he lashed himself to the helm. His eyes are wide open, transfixed with horror. When the harbormaster bends over him, he discovers two small bite marks on his neck.

In the background the gentlemen from customs have made their way into the cabin and the cargo bay. Rats scurry across the deck. A customs inspector comes to the harbormaster; he has found the ship's log. He reports that there is not a soul on board, and not much cargo. The cargo bay is full of rats, but the log was unharmed.

Wismar, Port Authority, Great Hall

All the officers of the port authority have gathered in the great hall, and with them the members of the town council. Some are wearing their official garb with their chains of office. A very dignified scene. The hall has generous proportions and displays various insignia of the Hanseatic League. A carved ship's prow has been mounted on the gable end, and the other decoration includes models of tall ships and schooners, anchors, and large paintings of ships contending with fierce storms.

The dead captain of the *Contamana* is lying in repose on a draped platform. A cross has been placed between his folded hands, and he is being shown nautical honors. Dr. Van Helsing is examining the dead man. He has discovered the bite marks on his neck but can make no sense of them. He is mystified, he admits, but perhaps the log can provide some insight.

The harbormaster, who together with some members of the council has leafed through the log, now begins to read: "Varma, 6 June. Crew, not counting me, the captain: two mates, five sailors, one cook. Departure for the Dardanelles . . ." He skips a few pages. "Course westerly . . . today the third sailor died of the fever. Last night the second mate, on duty at the helm, disappeared, leaving no trace. . . . 20 June: northerly course, Biscay, sea rough, 14 knots. . . . It is becoming ever more uncanny on board. Only the first mate and I remain alive. Something seems to be on board with us. Rats everywhere . . . can it be the plague?"

Horrified at the thought, the harbormaster breaks off. Around him the councilmen are struck dumb. Into the silence a shout rings out: plague! Consternation spreads through the assembled company; all those present want to make a dash for the exit. The harbormaster's voice calls on those who have lost their heads to pull themselves together, then go home quietly and lock their doors and windows.

Wismar, Harbor, the *Contamana,* Day

The ship lies motionless; nothing stirs. On deck all is still. There! Something is moving in the hatch to the cargo bay. Rats! They spill out of the cargo bay, out of the captain's cabin, out of every corner. They scurry, now forming a stream, over the gangplank onto dry land. They scramble along the anchor rope onto the dock. More and more of them appear. They are inquisitive, they are hungry, they sniff at everything.

Wismar, Small Town Square, Day

The streets are deserted, all the doors have been boarded up, and the shutters are closed. On one side of the small square we see a lovely, quiet canal and a bower-like roof of chestnut foliage overhanging it. The trees' spreading limbs make the peacefulness especially idyllic. From one side rats creep into view, sniffing. They form a broad phalanx, their numbers in the thousands.

Wismar, Streets, Night

We see a lonely street, lined with comfortable burghers' houses. All is still. From the shadow of a chestnut tree the figure of Nosferatu, silhouette-like, emerges into the moonlight. He is carrying a coffin. He takes a few stealthy steps, then pauses before disappearing down a side street.

The street where Harker's house is located. Not a soul to be seen, all the shutters closed up tight. Nosferatu comes with his coffin and disappears into the old, partial ruin of a house diagonally across from Harker's. Darkness stares from the black holes of the windows. Nothing stirs, not a sound.

Wismar, Harbor, Night

On the deserted dock stand four or five coffins. Nosferatu hurries down the gangplank with an air of uncanny busyness and deposits another coffin. Then he disappears onto the ship again.

Wismar, Cemetery, Night

A strange, silent cemetery on which the moon is shining. Nosferatu sneaks in with a coffin and makes straight for a small, tumbledown chapel, into which he disappears. Moments later he reappears, without the coffin. Is he creating hiding places for himself?

Landscape near Wismar, Morning

A causeway that divides a lake in half; islands, trees. As in an old painting a carriage approaches, reflected in the water along with the trees that line the causeway. Birds chirp, the horses' hooves clatter, the horses snort.

Wismar, Schrader's House, Morning

On the deserted street, where not a soul can be seen far and wide, the coach stops in front of Schrader's house. Two men and the coachman help a sick man out. They have to hold him up. He has blankets draped over his shoulders. Not until they ring the bell several times does Mina hesitantly open the door.

Closer up. The coachman is about to launch into an explanation when Lucy joins her sister-in-law at the door. Madam, he begins, saying that they are bringing this man because apparently he belongs here. Lucy has recognized Jonathan instantly and throws herself at him with a cry. She is beside herself with joy. Jonathan looks ill and disheveled; confused and repelled he frees himself from Lucy's embrace and looks at the coachmen in bewilderment. Who in the world is this woman? he asks. That is too much for Lucy. She steps back, making a strange groping gesture behind her, and falls in a faint. Schrader, who has just joined the women at the door, catches her in his arms.

Wismar, Schrader's House, Interior, Day

In the spacious parlor in Schrader's house Mina and Schrader are attending to Lucy; in time of need the members of the family look after each other. Van Helsing is with the ailing Jonathan, who has been wrapped in blankets and settled half-reclining in a comfortable armchair. The armchair stands near the window. Now that he has concluded his examination, Van Helsing packs up several instruments. He ventures a guess that Jonathan is suffering from a severe case of brain fever. Jonathan grows agitated, covering his eyes with his hand and muttering that the sun hurts him.

On a signal from Van Helsing, Schrader helps him push the armchair into the darkest corner of the room. There the patient seems to feel better. Mina and Lucy close the curtains. Outside the canal lies in bright morning sun. Lucy turns to Van Helsing and abruptly and almost rudely asks him whether he considers it possible that they might all have gone insane, and, upon coming to their senses one day, might find themselves all in straitjackets.

Wismar, Alley, Day

We see a quiet alley, paved with cobblestones, in a burghers' neighborhood. The idyllic houses all have their shutters and doors boarded up, however. Suddenly, like a torrent of water, rats come running toward us, filling the entire width of the alley. And now the spring flood has arrived: thousands of rats, all running in the same direction.

Another alley, with several steps leading down. We see a man fleeing. Behind him, rats cascade like a waterfall. And now from the opposite direction streams another flood of rats, surrounding him.

A quiet canal with a still, lovely roof of leaves overhead. The water does not move. But across the bridge something flows, a stream of rats.

Wismar, Harbor, Day

On the dock a man is trapped in a flood of rats. He has no idea what to do. He sees a hawser that has been used to moor a ship.

The man begins to swing hand-over-hand along the hawser toward safety on the ship.

We see his hands on the rope. But creeping along the rope behind him come the rats. And there! From the other end, from the ship, suddenly rats come toward his hands. His hands let go and the man plummets into the water. At the spot where he was holding the rope, the two streams of rats meet. The leaders of the two columns sniff each other with curiosity.

Wismar, outside Harker's House, Night

The windows in Harker's house that overlook the street are brightly lit. The sound of soft footsteps. Then a long shadow falls on the house. The large ears and claw-like hands tell us at once that Nosferatu is coming. The vampire steps out of the darkness and sniffs the air. He peers into the well-lit parlor. Following his gaze, we see Jonathan sitting apathetically in his armchair, as well as Lucy, Mina, Schrader, and Van Helsing. Lucy is holding Jonathan's journal, and apparently they are discussing it, but we do not hear what is said inside the room.

Lucy seems distraught because the others in the room cannot follow her thinking, or do not wish to. She takes the journal and lays it on the table in front of Van Helsing, pointing out a specific passage to him. Sinister and motionless, Nosferatu watches every move inside the room. He is biding his time. Silence.

Inside, Van Helsing, Schrader, and Mina have risen to take their leave. Nosferatu slips into the shadows as the door opens and footsteps are heard. The footsteps of the three die away.

Wismar, Harker's House, Interior, Night

The bedchamber. Lucy sits before the mirror preparing for bed. She has already put on her nightgown and let down her hair. Around her neck she wears a small silver cross. Her kitten is playing nearby on a chair upholstered in velvet. Lucy is very composed.

Suddenly Lucy's kitten undergoes a strange transformation. She is the first to notice something amiss. Every hair in her coat stands on end, and she arches her back and hisses in the direction of the door. The door creaks slightly, then opens as if of its own accord. Silently, like a ghost, Nosferatu suddenly appears in the room, his face ecstatic at the prospect of prey. He sneaks up on Lucy. All at once she senses the proximity of danger, looks at the kitten, and with a slight turn of her head discovers the interloper behind her. A glance back into the mirror makes her even more terrified, for she can see herself, but the vampire behind her has no reflection.

He realizes his mistake and takes a step to one side, as if to make sure that he cannot appear in the mirror. A terrible knowledge comes over Lucy. Nosferatu begins to speak, softly, asking her to pardon him for not announcing his visit in advance; he is Count Dracula. She knows about him, Lucy says bravely, for she has read Jonathan's journal. Jonathan has been done for since visiting him, she continues. He will not die, Dracula says. Yes, he will, says Lucy, Death is great, and all of us belong to him. The rivers can flow without us, time passes, and—let him just look outside—the stars drift toward us, confused. Only Death's cruelty is certain. Dying, Nosferatu says, is cruel to those not in the know, but Death is not the worst; much worse is being unable to die. He wishes, he says lasciviously, he could share in the love that exists between her and Jonathan. Nothing in the world, Lucy responds, can touch that love, even if since his return Jonathan no longer recognizes her. He, the vampire, has the power to change everything, he says imploringly; she should come to him, become his ally; that can mean salvation for her husband, and also for him. The absence of love, that she should know herself, is the greatest source of pain.

Gradually Lucy sheds her fear. She feels strangely drawn to the nocturnal visitor. The vampire approaches Lucy covetously. His face assumes a suffering, profoundly sorrowful expression. He reaches for her. Lucy recognizes the danger in the situation. She straightens up and takes a step that brings her close to the vampire. Her action bespeaks boldness. They alone, she says, hold the key to salvation. She uncovers the silver cross on her breast, and the vampire recoils. And he should feel certain, she adds, that she is not afraid to contemplate even that which seems most improbable. Good night.

Nosferatu backs away, retreating from the protective spell of the silver crucifix, which fills him with repulsion. With a groan and a quick turn into the darkness he disappears into the shadows outside the open door.

Lucy's kitten close up. She calms down fairly quickly, her coat smoothing out, and just hisses a few more times in the direction of the door. Then she goes back to playing her charming, silly games.

Insane Asylum, Renfield's Cell

Renfield is huddled on his cot as usual, paying no attention to what takes place around him. He watches the attendant drowsily as he sweeps his cell. For a moment the attendant steps out into the corridor to fetch a bucket. At a single bound Renfield leaps off the bed and takes cover behind the door. The attendant returns unsuspectingly, the bucket in his hand, and at the door Renfield jumps him from the side and goes straight for his neck.

The attendant falls to the ground, and for a moment Renfield cannot decide whether he should bite his neck or flee. Then, with a grotesque leap, he takes to his heels. He bangs the cell door shut and turns the key from the outside. The attendant scrambles to his feet and flings himself against the door, but it is too late; he is locked in.

Wismar, a Street

A street devoid of people, only pigeons on the pavement. At one house's front door stands an open coffin, empty, and next to it a plague wagon with a weary, emaciated horse. Renfield appears. He dashes past with an odd, hopping gait and disappears down an alley.

Wismar, Harker's Residence

Lucy stands at the window looking out. To one side of her Jonathan mutters feverishly that the coffins should be stopped. We follow Lucy's gaze and catch sight of a municipal employee, a small man all in black—a solemn but slightly shabby frock coat and a tall top hat. The man hobbles to every door and knocks. At the first door he listens. He knocks again, but nothing stirs inside. The man makes a large cross in white chalk on the door. Then the next. Again, no response and another cross. The occupants are dead. At the next door he again receives no answer. The man is just about to make the cross on the door when it opens a crack and a woman, clearly ailing, peers out timidly. She promptly closes the door again. No cross. The crooked little man continues on his way, listens at the next door, knocks . . .

Lucy turns away from the window and takes a seat very close to Jonathan. She picks up the book on vampires that was lying open on a little reading table. She begins to read: "Nosferatu, the undead. He drinks his victims' blood and turns them into ghosts of the night. He is like a shadow and has no reflection in mirrors. When night falls, he sallies forth in search of prey and forces his way through outer and inner walls and doors. He floats in the shape of a bat into the rooms of sleepers; as a black wolf he pursues those who attempt to flee. When he comes, all hope is lost . . ."

Lucy lowers the book to her lap for a moment because she has noticed that Jonathan, sitting next to her, has been listening more and more intently to every word. He seems to perk up immensely. He laughs out loud, then stops himself. Lucy tries to control her consternation. She skips a few pages but keeps an eye on Jonathan. She resumes reading: "He rules over all sorts of creatures, among them rats, bats, and wolves. Graves are his place of residence, especially the burial grounds for victims of the plague. And yet, although the vampire is an unnatural being, he must nonetheless obey certain laws of nature. The sign of the cross can stop him. A ray of sun destroys him. A holy wafer can make his hiding place uninhabitable. When a woman pure of heart causes him to miss the cock's crow, the light of day proves his undoing . . ."

Wismar, Square, toward Evening

The main square of Wismar. Striding purposefully, Lucy arrives and enters the square, lined with handsome burghers' houses. At one end stands the tall Gothic town church, at the other the richly ornamented town hall. We see a grisly procession coming toward Lucy, a long line of coffins, each borne on the shoulders of four men. All the pallbearers are dressed in black and wear top hats. The line stretches to the end of the square.

The lead pallbearer shouts at Lucy from a distance of several meters that she should stay away; the plague is here, and why would she want to be anywhere in the vicinity? She must get to the town council, Lucy replies. The council has dissolved itself, it no longer exists, the man tells her. Then she must see the burgomaster, Lucy insists. He is dead, the man says, and she should go home at once. Lucy tries to explain that she knows the source of all the evil, but no one heeds her explanation, and the procession moves on. Lucy is desperate but realizes that it is pointless; no one here wants to listen. She turns back.

A Field, Night

On a moonlit field outside the town, as clouds scud across the sky, Nosferatu and Renfield have found each other. They are standing at the fork of two lanes. Nearby cows are pastured. The cows raise their heads and eye the two figures in silence. The two are whispering. Renfield asks deferentially what orders his master has for him. He should go north, to Riga, Nosferatu says. May the army of rats and the black death be with him. Let his, Nosferatu's, will be done, Renfield exclaims. Amen, amen, amen, amen.

He sets out and disappears from our sight. Nosferatu turns and approaches the cows. A gesture from the vampire, and they fall into epileptic raving. Then the cows go into convulsions. The vampire vanishes into the nocturnal darkness. In the sky, stark against the shimmering moon, we see the shadow of an enormous bat.

Wismar, the Harker House, Parlor, Day

Lucy is sitting with Van Helsing in a corner of the parlor. She pleads with the doctor with great fervor but speaks softly to prevent Jonathan in the background from hearing her. He is sleeping fitfully in his armchair. The curtain at the window next to him is partly drawn to shield him from the sunlight outside. Van Helsing closes the vampire book and pushes it away, commenting that its contents are the spawn of imagination gone wild. This comment merely heightens Lucy's urgency; she reminds him that he has read Jonathan's journal and seen everything with his own eyes. Out in the town the situation with the rats and the plague worsens from one day to the next, and the full explanation can be found in this book about vampires. Van Helsing tries to calm her, expostulating that they live in an enlightened age, an age when science has banished such superstitions. No, Lucy replies, her certainty burns within her; she believes that which she has witnessed with her own eyes. That is mere belief, Van Helsing says. Yes, belief, Dr. Van Helsing, Lucy insists: belief is the remarkable human capacity that makes it possible to see things commonly held to be untrue. He should help her destroy the monster, she says. They would have to find where he hides out; coffins arrived with the ship from the Black Sea. The two of them should get to work this very evening. She needs peace and rest, Van Helsing replies; the ordeal with her husband has indubitably affected her; the whole business must first be examined scientifically. No, says Lucy, becoming ever more insistent, they must begin this very night; there is no time to be lost. Van Helsing puts his hand reassuringly on Lucy's shoulder, reminding her that a good farmer knows that everything takes time; it would never occur to such a farmer to dig up the wheat to see whether the roots were growing. Only children playing at being farmers would do such a thing.

Lucy despairs of persuading Van Helsing. She falls silent, but she feels her courage growing within her. She will destroy the monster herself then, she tells the doctor. With a curt bow Van Helsing takes his leave and departs. Lucy tiptoes over to Jonathan, who has woken up. She lovingly brushes his damp hair from his forehead and straightens his pillow. Jonathan looks at her in astonishment, a vague memory struggling to come to the surface. Mother Superior, he says, my medicine. And then he wonders aloud how he comes to know this lady.

Wismar, Dracula's House, Night

The night is stormy. A shutter on the crumbling house into which Dracula has moved creaks on its hinges and bangs against the house wall as it swings back and forth in the wind. Lucy appears, striding purposefully. The ground is swarming with rats; there are more here than anywhere else. With one hand Lucy holds her shawl together as it billows in the storm, while in the other she carries a lantern. Her gait tells us that she is prepared for the utmost. She finds the front door unlocked and enters without hesitation.

Dracula's House, Interior, Night

The door slams shut behind Lucy of its own accord. So this is the monster's house. The ground is littered with debris; in some places there are no upper floors and also no roof, so one can see straight up to the gloomy night sky. Rats scurry around. There is junk in some of the rooms, but otherwise the house seems like a ruin into which it has rained for years on end.

Another room. Lucy forges ahead, determined. The steps to the cellar. Lucy lights them with her lantern while fumbling at her neck to bare the silver crucifix, by which she feels protected. She gropes her way down the stairs. Everything is damp and moldy. There, in a corner, rats dart to take cover behind something long and black. It is what Lucy has been looking for: a coffin. The lid is slightly off-kilter. Lucy lifts it entirely, prepared for the worst. But the coffin is empty except for some black earth. Lucy removes a white holy wafer from a pocket, crumbles it with her fingers, and drops the crumbs into the coffin.

Wismar, Town Square, Early Morning

The air is filled with a wondrous, otherworldly singing. We survey the entire square, which has undergone a remarkable transformation. Furniture is piled up out in the open; people have divested themselves of all superfluous possessions. Bonfires crackle. There are stacks of coffins. Cattle roam about. A man is roasting a pigeon over coals. He is wearing a frock coat, but his gestures evoke Neanderthal man. His top hat reflects the glow of the fire. Another man is sitting on a bridge, counting his money into the water. A sheep wanders around amid plush sofas. The houses are boarded up, and whatever life remains has moved out into the open. A woman sits motionless in an armchair. Two large sows trot by. A flagellant monk harangues all who will listen. Rats atop wine barrels, coffins, wooden crucifixes. A broken-down coach with the cadaver of its horse still in the traces. The luggage has tumbled off the roof, and suitcases have split and lie strewn about. Another monk, dead drunk, is snoring at the entrance to the church. Two men, as naked as the day they were born, dash through the square, plunge into a canal, and swim for all they are worth.

From high in the church tower we gaze over the entire town and down into the square. Any semblance of order has collapsed, and the square is thronged with people. The singing in the air intensifies. Down below people are dancing. The town is beginning to lose its moorings.

Astonished, Lucy comes onto the square. Men are creating a huge pile of valuable furniture out in the open. An inebriated monk staggers by. Catch the foxes for us, the little foxes who are ruining the vineyards, he says, for the vineyards have grown eyes. An older man takes Lucy by the arm and pulls her into a round dance. A man with a fiddle accompanies the dance. Another man is blowing a mournful French horn. A child has hitched a large rooster to a small cart. Fires smolder. Lucy frees herself, but a sheep blocks her way. The entire square is dancing—children, widows, monks. People are picnicking on the coffins. A large round table has been spread with wine, food, a suckling pig. The fiddler plays for dear life. Herr Henning is dancing on the table with a ram. Someone hands Lucy a goblet of wine.

In one corner of the square a large table has been set with the finest porcelain. The town's elite are seated there. Choice wines, damask napkins, silver platters piled high with delicacies. Here the rats have formed enormous clumps, and the entire company is surrounded by a surging sea of rats. They are also creeping around on the table. But the diners seem completely unperturbed. Flowery table talk, the most refined manners. With a delicate gesture a lady removes a rat from her plate. Lucy approaches and is immediately invited to join them for a glass of wine. All of them have the plague, the imbibers tell her, so now they intend to enjoy life's gifts to the fullest. The singing in the air persists. We turn and look directly into the sun.

Harker Residence, Bedchamber, Day

Lucy is on her bed, sleeping out of sheer exhaustion. Next to her lies Jonathan, tossing and turning. The curtain is slightly open, and a streak of daylight shines into the room. On Lucy's breast we spy the little silver crucifix. She is breathing deeply and evenly. At the front door a racket is heard, and someone knocks and rattles the door. A woman's voice calls out that Madame Lucy should open the door, quickly! Lucy sits bolt upright and tears back the curtain. Daylight streams in. Jonathan wakes up as well but is terribly weak and feverish. Now we can see unmistakably two fresh bite marks on his neck.

Lucy pulls on her dressing gown. Already footsteps can be heard in the house. When Lucy opens the door of the bedchamber, she sees the maidservant from Schrader's house standing there. Is Lucy unharmed? the woman asks. She should come at once to Schrader's house; something terrible has happened.

Wismar, Street, Day

The maidservant and Lucy hasten through the town. The morning is deceptively quiet, with not a soul out and about. People have barricaded themselves indoors; even the mild light of day can no longer conceal the town's loss of its moorings. Lucy has dressed in great haste. Her hair is still loose.

Wismar, Schrader Residence

The Schrader household is in a complete uproar. Servants rush about like headless chickens. A police clerk is taking notes. Two attendants from the insane asylum have forced a man into a straitjacket. They have him prone on the ground and are tying the sleeves behind his back. When they turn him over, Lucy recognizes her brother-in-law, Schrader, who stares at her dementedly. He is foaming at the mouth. The next thing Lucy sees roots her to the spot in horror. Mina is stretched out on the floor, white as a sheet and dead. She is still wearing her lace-trimmed nightgown. Traces of blood on her neck. Van Helsing is bending over her. He straightens up and tells Lucy to compose herself. She should feel free to approach: it is clearly not the plague. Lucy struggles to ask what happened; how could God be indifferent to something like this? Nothing is known for certain, Van Helsing replies. Schrader found Mina dead this morning, and that caused him to lose his reason and begin to rave. The servants were unable to calm him. It must be some form of madness that has come over him. And Mina? Lucy asks, adding that it is all clear to her now. The causes will have to be determined scientifically, Van Helsing declares, by methods free of all prejudice and superstition. But already the plague can be excluded as a cause. By the by, the plague has now spread to the towns along the Baltic coast and is said to have reached Riga. Enough, Lucy says, enough of this scientific approach. She knows now what she must do.

Wismar, Harker Residence, toward Evening

Lucy has dressed in her Sunday best. She stands before the mirror and takes a long look at herself. Then she carefully removes the silver crucifix from her neck and places it in a drawer. She is ready.

Once more she picks up the book on vampires. It is closed, but a bookmark has been placed to mark a passage. Lucy opens the book and quickly reviews the words: "A ray of sun destroys him. . . . When a woman pure of heart causes him to miss the cock's crow, the light of day proves his undoing . . ." She closes the book firmly; she has made her decision. A clock in the house strikes seven.

Lucy returns to Jonathan and settles him for the night in his armchair; she wants to be alone in the bedchamber. She bends over him and gives him a loving kiss. Jonathan's face shows signs of life; suddenly he stares strangely at Lucy's white neck, but she does not notice. Lucy closes the draperies and leaves the room— as if it were an ordinary evening.

Wismar, Dracula's House, Evening

The vampire's ghostly house stands unchanged as evening falls. All is still. Something flutters out through one of the empty windows. A bat? After that, nothing stirs for a long time.

Wismar, Harker Residence, Night

Lucy stands at a window in her own house, gazing out. She stands there and waits. She has opened the draperies. A black bat has glued itself to a windowpane and stares boldly into the room.

The bed is made. White roses have been placed in a vase, and white rose petals have been strewn over the floor and bed. Candles burn in a candelabrum. A solemn feeling fills the room, somehow festive. Lucy has arranged everything, and she looks calm and lovely. Then something occurs to her. She goes across the hall to the parlor, where Jonathan is already asleep in his armchair. Lucy fetches a holy wafer from a little box and crumbles it. She spreads the crumbs in a circle around Jonathan. May God protect him, she murmurs, and keep him unharmed.

The house lies quiet in the quiet street on the quiet canal. Two windows of the bedchamber are lit from within, and we see Lucy waiting. She is ready. The bell in a church tower slowly strikes twelve. The sound echoes for a long time.

Wismar, Dracula's House, Night

Our gaze remains fixed on the half-ruined house with its gaping empty window openings. For a long time nothing moves. Then Nosferatu suddenly appears at one of the windows. Slowly he stretches to his full height, his face chalky white and profoundly mournful. His eyes go to Lucy's windows. Moving deliberately, the vampire steps away from his window and makes his way to the front door of his house. He glides along like a silhouette. Then his front door opens, and from the dark doorway the vampire's figure emerges. His ears seem to have become even larger flaps, his fingers longer claws. Without a sound he approaches; he is coming.

Wismar, Harker Residence, Bedchamber, Night

Lucy is lying on her bed in her silk nightgown among the white rose petals. The vampire approaches the bed, his clawed arms raised above his head like wings, his shadow at his feet. Lucy lies there expectantly, in almost trancelike surrender. The vampire bends over her, bringing his face very close to hers. Lucy becomes deathly afraid and tries to hold him off with her hands. The vampire, pushed away, sighs deeply, his face expressing unbelievable suffering. Slowly Lucy lowers her arms and offers her body, which takes on a seductive, erotic aura. The vampire, sighing, gazes at her and pushes her nightgown up to her thighs. He feels her body and sniffs the air. Slowly he turns his attention to her neck, which she likewise offers him. The vampire sinks his teeth into her throat and sucks and sucks. Lucy places her arms around him. The candles begin to flicker, and in the uncertain light we see the shadows of black bats. The flickering increases.

Visions

The fluttering of the bats, tracing a jerky zigzag against the dark sky, becomes a slow, majestic beating of wings. The bats fly like herons. Their mouths open wide to emit a soundless cry. On the ocean, the waves are whipped by a storm, and a dark ship sails toward us from the horizon.

A subterranean canal. A large, crab-like creature with a human face dips its pincer-like arms into the slow-flowing water and stares at us boldly. The terrifying man-sized animal moves its antennae ever so slightly, picking up our presence; it stares rigidly at us.

In a dark corridor stands a gigantic spider, dark and menacing, as large as a person. It too has picked us up on its antennae, and slowly it raises its two front legs.

Then comes another long, dim corridor. On both walls mummies are lined up, all with mouths gaping open, a mighty chorale. The mummified corpses lean against the walls to the left and right, like boards stored upright. The sight is grisly. Many of the mummies are wearing dusty, moth-eaten clothes, and some are completely naked. A young woman has nothing on but delicate shoes. Her skin is brownish, like parchment. Some of the bodies have partially fallen apart, but their postures and expressions remain distinct. They include men, women, and many children. Their gestures are natural, not arranged postmortem. The most horrible features are the open mouths. They stand there like a chorus of ghosts from whom another sound will nevermore be heard.

Wismar, Canal, toward Morning

Morning is on its way. The first light creeps along the horizon. A still canal lies cold and shrouded in fog in the morning air. The scene looks elegiac. A clock in a tower strikes four.

Wismar, Harker Residence, toward Morning

On the bed lies Lucy, half-unconscious. Bent over her neck the vampire, motionless for a long time, as spiders hold still when sucking the blood from their prey. Then Nosferatu slowly raises his satiated, satisfied face from Lucy's neck. His head and his eyelids look heavy. We see his long, pointed incisors. The vampire sniffs the air, looks toward the window, and catches sight of the first gleam of the dawning day. Slowly and sluggishly he tries to rise. At that, Lucy's arms lovingly encircle him and draw him gently down to her. After a moment of hesitation the vampire, like an infant who has had his fill, nonetheless succumbs to drinking once more. Lucy holds him tightly.

Wismar, View of the Town, Early Morning

The morning sun has already reached the top of the high church tower and is working its way slowly downward. The first gables of the surrounding houses are dipped in reddish light. A great stillness prevails. Then, into the stillness, a cock crows. At a distance, a second cock crows in reply.

Wismar, Harker Residence, Morning

Lucy remains in the same posture on her bed. Now she is white as snow, almost transparent. Nosferatu is still at her neck, motionless, still drinking a little from her. From outside the cock's crow is heard. Suddenly wide awake, the vampire pricks up his ears. Sensing danger, he raises his head and turns toward the window. The houses across the way are already bathed up to their attics in the light of the morning sun. Abruptly the vampire lets go of Lucy and steps to the window to look out. We see him from behind, from very close up. He lingers for a moment at the window, suddenly realizing the danger. Then a ray strikes him at an angle. The vampire twitches, his body convulses, then goes into contortions like that of someone pierced with a spear. Slowly he turns. His face is terribly distorted from the light, his eyes empty. Unseeing, he stares into the room, only the whites showing. He stands there, wracked with terrible spasms, for seconds that seem to last an eternity. Then he collapses.

Lucy tries to sit up on her bed, but she is too greatly weakened. She sinks back onto her pillow and dies, an expression of happiness on her face. On the floor Nosferatu perishes in gruesome contortions.

Wismar, Harker Residence, Exterior, Day

It is a bright, sunny day. At the entrance to Harker's house a crowd of the curious has gathered, but they do not have the courage to cross the threshold. Everyone is waiting, trying to catch a glimpse of what is apparently happening inside. The crowd waits in silence, like people witnessing a terrible accident.

Wismar, Harker Residence, Interior, Day

The bedchamber. Dr. Van Helsing, his face ashen, is bending over Lucy. Now he straightens up and carefully folds her hands. On the floor, horribly contorted, lies Nosferatu. Now he sees it all, the doctor murmurs, oh my God, if only he had listened to her before. Quick, bring a stake and a hammer, so he can destroy the monster once and for all.

The parlor. Jonathan wakes up, clear in the head now, and stretches. Van Helsing rushes past him, carrying a stake, pointed at one end, and a heavy hammer into the bedchamber. We hear dull hammer blows. The blows go through Jonathan as if he himself were being struck. He jumps up and wants to follow the sound, but the sacred circle holds him captive. He cannot move beyond his chair. On all sides he bumps into something that stops him. He howls like an animal. When he opens his mouth, we see that he has two long, pointed incisors, like a rodent. He cries for help.

Tumult arises in the corridor—footsteps, shouts, the door opens, and about ten people hurtle into the room. There is Dr. Van Helsing, Jonathan shouts, arrest him! Van Helsing is just coming from the bedchamber with the hammer in his right hand. He is spattered with blood, having carried out his gruesome task. He should be taken prisoner, Jonathan repeats; he just murdered someone, the Count. Several officials have made their way into the bedchamber. One official approaches Van Helsing and asks whether he was the one who drove this stake through the Count's heart. Yes, Van Helsing confirms, but he has an important explanation to provide. He needs no explanation, the official replies icily; he, Dr. Van Helsing, is under arrest. Arrest him, he orders the crooked little municipal employee whom we met when he was chalking crosses on doors. Arrest? the man repeats in perplexity, his voice raspy. He should fetch the police, the official snaps at him. The entire police force is dead, the man replies. Then he should take the doctor to prison, barks the official. The prison guards are no longer alive, the crooked little man says in growing desperation. Then he should carry out the arrest himself, shouts the official. But he is unarmed; he would need to be armed, and he has never arrested anyone, writhes the little man. Where do they want to take him? Dr. Van Helsing interjects. Well, the public servant stammers, that he does not know himself, and he leads him away. Van Helsing goes quietly and without resisting. Most of the curiosity seekers follow them out of the house. Only Jonathan, a maidservant, and several burghers remain. Jonathan has somewhere he wants to go, but he cannot move. He turns to the maid and orders her to fetch a broom; the place is full of dust. The maid fetches a broom and dustpan and begins sweeping. No sooner are the crumbs from the wafer swept away than Jonathan steps forward boldly. His face is immobile and white, his voice almost without resonance. He orders the bedchamber to be sealed for inspection by the police and calls for his horse to be brought; he has much to do.

Vast Seashore, Day

The roar of a storm is in the air, the sky is overcast, sand whips along the ground toward us. The clouds are racing. Like a storm, a rider on a black horse gallops into sight. His coat flutters behind him. It is Jonathan. He gallops past, his face rapturous. He disappears over the horizon. All that remain are the crazed clouds, hurtling across the darkened sky.

Where the Green Ants Dream

For your mine you have torn up the land; don't you see
that you are tearing up my body as well?

—SAM WOOLAGOODJA, COCKATOO ISLAND,
NORTHWESTERN AUSTRALIA

CHARACTERS

LANCE HACKETT	*geologist, seismologist, employed by Ayers Mining Company Pty. Ltd.*
BANDHARRAWUY	*Aboriginal of the Riratjingu clan, Keeper of the Songs*
MILIRITBI	*oldest tribal elder of the Riratjingu clan*
BALDWIN FERGUSON	*executive vice president, Ayers Mining*
COLE	*foreman, Ayers Mining*
MISS STREHLOW	*widow with a dog*
ERNEST FLETCHER	*biologist, studies green ants*
ARNOLD	*former anthropologist*
BLACKWELL	*judge, Supreme Court, Northern Territory*
COULTHARD	*Crown counsel*
KARRAWURRA	*"the Mute," last member of the Worora clan*
WATSON	*half-breed, allegedly a pilot*
FITZSIMMONS	*missionary*
DAISY BARUNGA	*young woman, Riratjingu clan*
PROFESSOR STANNER	*expert witness in court*

The Ants

The green ants remain motionless. They hold still, as if ants could hold their breath, as if they were dead. Only the cautious twitching of their antennae reveals that they are alive. The green ants are dreaming. Through their dreams they invoke whole worlds.

And we immediately notice something odd: all the ants are facing in the same direction, like an army of miniature soldiers; we have never seen ants behave this way. Their positions on the sandy soil are completely random, but as if drawn by strange magnetic forces they have paused in their busy scurrying, all seeming to listen in the same direction, as if their dreams could be heard. And so the ants remain motionless, two hundred thousand strong.

We strain our ears because a mysterious pulsating sound comes to us from a distance, a sound that makes the ants seem even more unreal. The deep, pulsating, strangely rhythmic tones seem to emanate from the very depths of the earth, from the region where the prehistoric and the unreal are locked in combat, poised to trigger earthquakes. Soon we will discover, however, that these tones come from Miliritbi, who is playing a drone pipe, a didgeridoo.

Then we hear, over a walkie-talkie, a voice that overlays itself upon the dreaming armies. The voice is somewhat distorted by static, but the instructions it issues come across distinctly and calmly. The quiet, collected voice belongs to Hackett.

HACKETT'S VOICE: How far along are you? Have you connected the blasting cable? . . . Cole, do you read me?

COLE'S VOICE: Roger, blasting cable connected.

HACKETT'S VOICE: All right, get your ass out of there. A hundred meters at least. I hate having to go through this whole rigamarole just to calibrate the new meter. Where are you now?

COLE'S VOICE: East of two-five-two.

HACKETT'S VOICE: All right, I'm going to let her rip. Meter running. Twenty seconds. Stamp on the ground once, real hard.

COLE'S VOICE: Okay, Lance.

HACKETT'S VOICE: You stamped twice, you bastard. This machine doesn't miss a thing. If you sneeze a thousand kilometers away, it shows up on the meter. Ten seconds. Test running. Keep your head down. Five, four, three, two, one, ignition.

During this entire exchange the armies of green ants have been listening, motionless, to their dreams. The terrible thunderclap of an explosion tears through everything and veritably sends us flying out of our seats, yet for a long, uncanny second the ant armies stay put, until the blast wave that follows the rumble of the explosion scatters them. Then a fearsome wave of dust and sand sweeps across the ground, covering everything before it settles. What remains is burning dust. What remains is not a single ant. What remains is a dreamless void, covered in dust.

COLE'S VOICE: Something awful's happened.

HACKETT'S VOICE: Are you hurt?

COLE'S VOICE: My Coke can got knocked over; I didn't see that till just now. The world's going dark. I'm a dead man!

Mobile Geological Station, Interior

The interior of a good-sized trailer packed to the gills with technical equipment. Monitors, cables, devices similar to meteorological instruments, fluorescent lights, a refrigerator. The most important device is a highly sensitive instrument that records everything, even almost imperceptible seismic variations. A wide strip of computer paper streams uninterruptedly out of the device, showing several parallel wavy lines that measure simultaneous oscillations at different locations. The paper folds itself in a fan as it lands in a rack. Above the door a bulky air conditioner that hums loudly and constantly drips condensed water.

Hackett is at work in the trailer. He is a youngish scientist with a sturdy build and measured gestures. He looks like someone who at one time might have played on New England's toughest ice hockey team, who was constantly being benched for fighting on the ice, who might have lost several teeth, collected scars, and baptized his teammates with beer in the locker room after a win. Yet his features have acquired an inward quality, a stillness, as if in one game, which would turn out to be his last, something terrible had happened, as if he had rammed a player from the opposing team so hard that from then on that player was paralyzed, confined to a wheelchair. For all his toughness Hackett looks vulnerable, and one can picture him lying awake for a long time at night, alone.

With him in the mobile station, somewhat in the background but instantly recognizable as out of place, is Miss Strehlow, a woman over seventy, her cheeks flushed with agitation. Under her kerchief we see the outlines of the curlers she never takes off, like the ring on her finger. She digs a Polaroid out of her pocketbook. Hackett has a small portable two-way radio in front of him on a narrow table, and he's holding the microphone that goes with it.

COLE'S VOICE: This heat is killing me. Do you have any idea how hot it is out here?

HACKETT: A bit over 104.

He leans toward the window to look at the thermometer screwed to the outside of the trailer.

HACKETT: Damn! A hundred eleven. And the air conditioner's not doing its job. Come inside; at least the Coke's keeping cold.

MISS STREHLOW: Ben. This is my Ben. Benjamin Franklin.

She holds up the Polaroid. She has been quiet for so long that she has to get Hackett's attention.

From outside the strange sounds of the didgeridoo make their way into the trailer.

Near Coober Pedy, Flinders Range Test Area, Claim 252
A wrecked construction crane, collapsed and abandoned in the dusty expanse of this godforsaken landscape. Several Aboriginals

are huddled in its shadow. The first person we notice is Miliritbi, who is playing the didgeridoo, a thick wooden pipe, very simple, without a mouthpiece of any kind. He takes quick breaths through his nose while keeping his cheeks constantly puffed out like a bagpipe player's to produce a sustained, pulsating drone. Miliritbi has tamed his wild hair somewhat with a frayed headband. He is wearing a faded shirt and wrinkled baggy pants, and he is barefoot like the others around him. On his wrist he has one of those cheap electric watches made of black plastic whose numerals have a reddish glow. Miliritbi's beard has already turned completely white, while his hair is still dark.

We also immediately notice Bandharrawuy, an extraordinarily dignified old man, the only man standing and holding a spear. All he wears is a pair of long pants, no shirt or shoes. On his chest we see a row of thick horizontal scars that goes all the way down to his belly, evidently originating in the male initiation rites of his youth. His right shoulder bears a brand scar the size of a small plate.

Squatting next to him on the ground is Karrawurra, the Mute, also an old man with a penetrating gaze. Several dogs are lounging around, half-asleep, their tongues hanging out as they try to cool themselves. Several more men huddle close to the wrecked crane. One of them has a cheap transistor radio with him, but it is turned off. Off to one side, Watson, a youngish half-breed, is leaning against the tangled system of rods that once operated the boom and drinking beer from a can. Near him are two women, the younger of whom is Daisy Barunga, a handsome girl with long limbs. Watson wears jeans and cowboy boots with stacked heels, and he has pulled his rakishly dented cowboy hat down almost to his eyebrows. He strikes a casual pose like the outlaws in *High Noon*.

Not far off, where the terrain rises slightly, we see a cluster of vehicles parked, among them several Land Rovers, a Caterpillar with a gigantic blade, and in their midst, like a white, rectangular block, the mobile geological station. The Land Rovers are also painted white and have the logo of the Ayers Mining Pty. Ltd. on their doors.

Beyond the seismological station a low, pyramid-shaped hill rises out of the desert sand. Below its peak, we see the mouths of tunnels drilled into the hill in concentric circles, and that lends the hill an almost human quality. It looks like the Man of Sorrows. Here and there we also see small, almost pure white heaps of tailings from the tunnels that trucks have dumped at random on the plain. Later we will see an entire landscape characterized by this feature.

The air above the entire scene shimmers with heat and haze. The Aboriginals are all staring in one direction—toward the place where the geological station was dropped, seemingly without forethought, on the plain. A wind gust swirls a cloud of dust, glowing with heat, into the air. The dogs stretch. The dust envelops everything, then settles. Cole, a bulky man with a thick neck and a face seamed by exposure to the elements, appears out of a long streamer of dust and heads toward Hackett's trailer like a man on a mission.

Mobile Geological Station, Interior

Looking somewhat at a loss but trying not to be rude, Hackett is holding Miss Strehlow's Polaroid. He has the air of an embarrassed schoolboy.

HACKETT: You know, Miss Strehler, we're . . .

MISS STREHLOW: Strehlow, it's Strehlow . . .

HACKETT: We're probably not the right ones to help you. Our seismometer, as you may have observed . . .

MISS STREHLOW: Footsteps . . . yes, and steps: the needle reacts, and Benny, my Ben . . .

She falls silent at the terrible things she is picturing and struggles to hold back tears.

MISS STREHLOW: . . . my Ben is wandering around inside the mountain, in the dark . . .

Cole enters without knocking and slams the door behind him before too much dust follows him in. The entire trailer shakes, and water spurts out of the malfunctioning air conditioner. The impact of Cole's entrance jolts Miss Strehlow into somewhat more rational territory.

COLE: A Coke! I'm dying.

He takes off his sweaty, dusty cap, wipes the accumulation of dust and encrusted spittle from the corners of his mouth, and pops open the can of Coke, beaded with cold moisture, that Hackett has fetched him from the refrigerator. As he opens the can, Cole contentedly scrunches it. With the steaming can he salutes Miss Strehlow, who has apparently got herself under control again.

COLE: Ma'am!

MISS STREHLOW: Mr. Hackett, could you show the young man the photo?

COLE: Hey, thanks! It's been a while since anyone's called me young man.

Hackett hands him the photo without comment. Cole takes a reflective gulp from the can.

MISS STREHLOW: That picture is four years old. Benny was only two then.

We see the photo from close up. Cole is holding it in his callused, freckled hands. We can make out Miss Strehlow holding a black cocker spaniel who is facing the camera. The photo must have been taken with a flash, to judge by the red glow of the dog's eyes.

MISS STREHLOW'S VOICE: When Mr. Franklin, God rest his soul, brought me the two pups, he asked me, Which one do you want, Lissy or Ben? and without a moment's thought I said, The little black one, he's so feisty and playful. My Ben.

She takes the photo from Cole and stows it in her pocketbook.

MISS STREHLOW: And because my neighbor's name was Franklin, I said, We'll call him Ben, but officially his first and last names are Benjamin Franklin. . . . You've got to find him!

Hackett does not know what to say. He looks to Cole for help, but Miss Strehlow refuses to let him off the hook.

HACKETT: You see, you're right that our apparatus picks up the smallest vibrations, even footsteps, but only when they happen right near one of our sensors.

The explanation raises Miss Strehlow's hopes; she seems almost relieved.

MISS STREHLOW: You're going to find Ben, my Ben.

HACKETT: Miss Strehlow, it doesn't work the way you think. Try to picture this: we bury sensors at precise intervals, and then we ignite our test explosions at precise intervals—and when I say precise, I mean with a tolerance of less than a ten-thousandth of a second. What we're actually measuring is the reverberation of these explosions from inside the earth. It's like an echo, and from slightly adjusted detonation events whose resonance is recorded we can establish a kind of profile of the strata deep underground . . .

MISS STREHLOW: But you also recorded footsteps . . .

HACKETT: As I said, that's possible. But if we apply this to your dog, we'd have to drill probes into the entire mountain and install sensors, and if we buried five thousand of them and by chance happened to put one within two meters of your dog, all he'd have to do would be to scratch himself behind the ear, and we'd know where he was . . .

MISS STREHLOW: Yes? Really?

HACKETT: You know what, Miss Strehlow? Your dog's going to find his way out of the mountain all by himself. Suddenly he'll be standing at the mouth of a tunnel and wagging his tail as if nothing happened.

MISS STREHLOW: Ben's never run away before, and the very first time he has to go into the mountain. And in there from one kilometer to the next it's worse than the worst labyrinth. And the darkness . . .

She swallows hard and stops in midsentence.

MISS STREHLOW: We've looked everywhere. My poor Ben.

Hackett pulls himself together, takes a step toward the old lady, and pats her reassuringly on the shoulder.

HACKETT: You know what? I'm going to drive you over to the village in my Land Rover. I have to go there anyway to let the team know we're ready to start.

Near Coober Pedy, Flinders Range, Claim 252

A Land Rover sets out from the mobile station, stirring up enormous plumes of dust in its wake. It heads toward the group of Aboriginals still huddled around the wrecked construction crane. In the Land Rover we see Miss Strehlow, holding a handkerchief over her mouth and nose to keep out the dust, which finds its way into the vehicle, and Hackett at the wheel. Hackett stops right beside Bandharrawuy and slides open the window on his side.

HACKETT: Hey there! You haven't exactly picked the most comfortable place to hang out.

For a moment a raging wind gust wraps everything in dust, and Hackett quickly slides the window shut again. He opens it a few minutes later, but this time he is careful to keep the opening small. The Aboriginals let the dust swirl over them; they do not move a muscle.

HACKETT: I think it would be better if you went somewhere else. We're going to be blasting shortly.

The faces of the Aboriginals. These faces convey incredible determination, almost hostility; something is up. Silence. A suspicion seems to dawn on Hackett.

HACKETT: You're never here normally. Only since we moved the trailer . . . Tell me, what are you folks up to?

Miliritbi turns to Bandharrawuy and speaks to him briefly in Riratjingu, a throaty, nice-sounding language. Bandharrawuy gives a brief answer. Miliritbi, who speaks English almost without an accent, translates.

MILIRITBI: We're keeping watch.

Silence. Nothing more is forthcoming from the Aboriginals. Only Watson, who seems to be quite drunk, raises his index finger, and, with a slow gesture intended to make an impression, pushes the brim of his cowboy hat up a bit higher on his forehead. He stares straight at Hackett, meanwhile using his tongue to shift a matchstick he was chewing on from one corner of his mouth to the other. Then, his eyes locked on Hackett's, he picks up an empty beer can from the sandy ground and, still staring at him, crushes it slowly in his fist. He is plainly enjoying this pantomime, which he knows is macho. At the very moment when he glances to one side to see whether he has made an impression on Daisy Barunga, a hot, stormy, seething wind gust wraps everything in dust.

Coober Pedy

We slowly scan the town of Coober Pedy, which does not actually exist because it consists only of widely scattered outskirts. There is no way to describe Coober Pedy other than as an insulted landscape. Many kilometers around the dusty desert have been dug into and churned up. The area's dimensions stagger the imagination, and staggering too are the small rocky elevations pockmarked with gaping tunnels. Prefabricated houses are scattered at random over the bleak terrain that was once a desert, and broken-down road construction equipment and even more broken-down drilling equipment have been left to rust where they were last used. Water tanks of corrugated tin painted white, television antennae, dust, and hopelessness, all of a desolation beyond anything the worst nightmares could conjure up. The settlement feels like something on an alien planet, established in irredeemable hideousness by alien, confused, dirty beings. Behind a battered fence we see junked cars piled high. There a dusty track comes to a dead end at a bench consisting of a car's back seat, its stuffing partially gone and the springs protruding—not exactly an inviting place to rest. Around it we see a ring of hundreds of empty beer cans. This must have been the throne of some wretched drinker. Behind the bench the countryside spreads in all directions to form a dreadful expanse, and we can picture this almost flat quasi-desert going on this way for hundreds and hundreds of kilometers. Dust swirls in long plumes across uncharted distances. In the middle of nowhere we see the screen of a drive-in movie theater that must have ceased operation years ago. Where the cars would have parked we see heaps of trash. Paper flutters over the deserted drive-in, a sign of its definitive end.

As far as the eye can see, tailings from the mines have been dumped wherever the trucks wanted to get rid of their loads: hundreds and thousands of cones of whitish sand dot the enormous plain. At first glance one can mistake the scene for the Janissaries' encampment of white and yellowish tents outside the gates of Vienna. Looking off in the distance, where heat flickers and everything seems to float away, one wonders: are those swans or snow? But we know it is the countless tents of the Ottomans.

The heat weighs heavily on the countryside. The sky, unrepentant as nowhere else, stares down hot and cloudless on the land as it is slowly incinerated. The land is vast and so wide that it hurts. And everywhere the sky is larger, even larger than the land.

Now several vehicles approach, emerging from a thick cloud of dust. We see two pickup trucks and an Ayers Land Rover. Workers wearing bright orange plastic hard hats are sitting in the beds of the pickups, hiding their faces in the crook of their elbows to protect themselves from the dust. The small convoy drives by, headed straight across the bleak terrain toward the mobile station.

Flinders Range Test Area, Claim 252

Now the Aboriginals are all on their feet, with the exception of Watson. They are gripped by uneasiness and stare in the direction of the mobile station.

The area around the station is a beehive of activity. For reasons that are not clear, one pickup keeps backing up. Workers in overalls and orange hard hats are stringing lightweight cables, which they unwind from portable spools. The activity focuses increasingly on a small rocky elevation that seems to have been spared any excavation up to this point. Several men, under the direction of Cole, the only one wearing a white hard hat, are carefully sinking a probe into a metal pipe that extends far down into the ground.

Mobile Station, Interior

Hackett works with deep concentration at a small, green-glowing monitor until he stabilizes a curve that was jumping up and down wildly. A workman in an orange hard hat opens the door briefly.

WORKMAN: Claim two-five-two ready for testing.

HACKETT: Thanks. I'll initiate in a moment.

The man hesitates in the doorway. Hackett notices and turns to look at him.

HACKETT: What's wrong?

WORKMAN: Sir, the boys outside wish you luck.

HACKETT: Thanks.

WORKMAN: The boys heard it was you who fought so hard with the company for the tests, I mean for getting the license for this area, and the boys . . .

Hackett seems to understand now. He smiles and picks up the microphone.

HACKETT: Cole, Cole, report!

COLE: Roger, over!

HACKETT: Get the boys out of range, and tell them there'll be champagne tonight. I'm willing to bet even before we run this test that we're sitting on something with Claim two-five-two that'll knock their socks off at headquarters. But I've already shot my wad with my predictions . . .

From outside men's voices cheering can be heard and applause being pounded with heavy tools on the beds of pick-ups.

COLE'S VOICE: Everything okay here. Let 'er rip.

HACKETT: Siren, please.

From outside the ugly, grating wail of a siren can be heard.

HACKETT: Test initiated. Apparatus running. Thirty seconds.

Flinders Range Test Area, Claim 252

The workmen have withdrawn behind a specific line. Some of them are squatting on the ground while others have gone down on one knee and propped a forearm on the other knee, leaning forward. All stare in the direction of the rocky elevation. The Aboriginals are showing signs of unusual tension. Bandharrawuy quickly says something to Miliritbi in their language. Then Hackett's voice can be heard, coming somewhat distorted from a small loudspeaker.

HACKETT'S VOICE: Twenty seconds. Boys, this is going to be something.

Dust blows. Silence. Terrible tension seizes hold of the Aboriginals.

HACKETT'S VOICE: Ten seconds . . . five, four, three, two, one, ignition.

Everything happens at once. Like a bomb striking its target, the first explosion shoots a mushroom cloud of dust and rocks into the sky, and then comes the second explosion, then the third. At the very moment when we realize that the explosions are heading straight for the rocky elevation, Bandharrawuy darts out of the shadow of the crane, and, spear at the ready, makes for the predictable path of the explosions.

Cole has jumped up, the first to recognize the danger.

COLE: Stop! Get back!!!

But Bandharrawuy rushes on, pushing aside Cole, who bravely tries to block his path. The fourth detonation occurs not far from the two men and almost knocks them to the ground. The two disappear completely in the dust raised by the explosion. Cole's voice from inside the dust cloud almost cracks.

COLE: Cap the cable! Unplug the cable!

Two workmen have reacted faster than the others. They hurl themselves at a cable reel, and just as they yank out a connector another detonation occurs. Then the scene falls silent. The other workers have all leapt to their feet in incredulous amazement. The silence continues. The Aboriginals stare as if they were somewhere else entirely. Slowly the dust settles.

From amid the dispersing plumes of gritty sand two figures emerge, Cole and Bandharrawuy. They face each other wordlessly, calm and collected, both clearly ready to commit murder.

Mobile Station, Interior

Hackett is confused. Silence from outside. The curve on the green monitor has flatlined. The paper continues to spill out of the printer, showing, however, no more peaks and valleys. Hackett reaches for the microphone.

HACKETT: What happened? The pulse generator cut out.

COLE'S VOICE: That was the boys, thank God. Come out here. Someone here's lost his freaking mind.

Flinders Range Test Area, Claim 252

Bandharrawuy and Cole are still facing each other, so close their bodies almost touch. Bandharrawuy is completely calm, almost relaxed, which infuriates Cole even more. Hackett rushes toward them. At almost the same moment Miliritbi and Karrawurra join the group.

COLE: He's lost his mind. He could have gotten himself and me killed.

The workmen crowd around, all somewhat unsure of themselves. Bandharrawuy chooses this moment to sit down tranquilly on the ground, placing his spear across his knees.

HACKETT: What's going on here? Who can explain to me why anyone would run right into the path of our test?

Bandharrawuy speaks briefly and softly in Riratjingu.

HACKETT: What did he say?

MILIRITBI: There's to be no dynamiting and no excavating here.

HACKETT: And may I ask why, gentlemen?

MILIRITBI: Because this is where the green ants dream.

COLE: Ants! Green ants, here? Why can't the fucking creatures do their dreaming somewhere else?

Silence comes over the scene. The two parties face each other with fixed stares. Hackett is the first to speak.

HACKETT: Easy, Cole. Boys: secure the ignition cable. I'll see whether I can get headquarters on the radio.

Mobile Station, Interior

Hackett enters the trailer and promptly reaches for his small two-way radio, switches to a different frequency, and speaks into the microphone.

HACKETT: Headquarters . . . headquarters, do you read me? This is Flinders Range Test Area, two-five-two . . .

WOMAN'S VOICE: Lance, is that you? This is Nancy . . .

HACKETT: Is Ferguson around? I need to speak to Ferguson.

WOMAN'S VOICE: He's not here; he's in Sydney.

HACKETT: Call him, then. It's urgent. He has to come, immediately.

WOMAN'S VOICE: Even if I can reach him, the earliest he can get there is tomorrow . . . is something wrong?

HACKETT: Yes, we have a problem here. Tell Ferguson he needs to alert Legal; we have something like what happened that time in the North, in Aurukun, when a couple of the blacks lost it.

From outside voices have become audible, growing increasingly agitated, as if a fight has broken out. Cole's voice can be made out in the din. Suddenly everything is quiet, then the loud roar of an engine starting up.

HACKETT: Tell him . . . hang on . . .

Hackett tugs the coiled cord of the microphone as far as he can and leans to look out the window to see what is going on.

HACKETT: Good Lord! . . . Ferguson has to get here immediately. Immediately . . . You hear, Nancy? . . .

But what Hackett sees leaves him no time to wait for an answer; he storms out of the trailer, leaving the radio on.

WOMAN'S VOICE: Lance . . . Lance! What's wrong? . . . Lance, do you read me? Flinders Test, report!

Flinders Range Test Area, Claim 252

It is obvious at a glance what is going on. The Aboriginals have sat down on the ground, and the gigantic Caterpillar, with Cole in the driver's seat, is headed straight for them. He is only a few meters away, and now he lowers the enormous blade to the ground. Hackett races toward him. The workmen in the orange hard hats, who have been standing around, unsure of what to do, scatter.

HACKETT: Cole!!!

COLE: Hold your horses: I'm going to fix this!

The blade digs into the desert floor and shoves a growing pile of sand and rocks toward the group of Aboriginals.

Hackett from close up. He is aghast. The workmen, although they are certainly a tough bunch, look horrified.

Bandharrawuy close up. He is in front of the group of Aboriginals. He is sitting cross-legged on the ground, his spear across his knees, and his eyes look stoic, almost detached, as they stare into the distance. Behind him and a bit to one side sit Karrawurra and Miliritbi. As the blade comes dangerously close, Watson abruptly stands up and moves out of the way. For a moment it looks as though the others might also give way in the face of the oncoming monster. Watson casually spits out his matchstick in the direction of the Caterpillar. He snaps his fingers, as if he were in a disco.

WATSON: My baby does the hanky panky . . . da-dum.

But Bandharrawuy does not budge. The gently moving pile of sand has reached him, the massively heavy blade scoops him up and rolls him gently into Miliritbi, who now also begins to roll with the sand.

We see Hackett pick up an iron pipe lying on the ground and brandish it threateningly at Cole, enthroned atop the Caterpillar.

HACKETT: Cole! You stop this minute!

But Cole just stares straight ahead and keeps the machine moving forward, slowly. At that Hackett lands a crashing blow with the pipe on the frame of the driver's seat. The blow leaves a deep dent in the aluminum. Cole stops the machine without favoring Hackett with so much as a glance. Hackett speaks softly, dangerously composed.

HACKETT: Turn that thing off or you're a dead man.

Cole switches off the engine, still without looking at Hackett. He smiles contemptuously.

HACKETT: The key.

Cole slowly pulls out the key, as if none of this had anything to do with him, and without looking tosses it on the ground in front of Hackett. He rises from the seat, stretches, yawns, and finally turns to Hackett.

COLE: So has everyone gone stark raving mad today? I could've taken care of this in thirty seconds, and no one would've come away with anything more than a few scratches.

Hackett is speechless. He wants to say something, but he cannot, so first he bends over and awkwardly picks up the key.

COLE: You're going to pay for this.

Hackett turns to the Aboriginals, who after being rolled two or three times have now sat down again, at most a meter from the Caterpillar's blade. Miliritbi begins to challenge the blade by playing his didgeridoo, his drone pipe. In his perplexity Hackett makes a somewhat awkward formal bow to the barefoot Aboriginals.

HACKETT: On behalf of the company, I'd like to apologize.

Bandharrawuy slowly turns toward Hackett and looks at him for a long time, but his eyes seem to go right through him. The drone of the instrument continues. Wind blows and dust swirls.

Coober Pedy, Early Morning

The settlement is still asleep. The bleak landscape lies in the pale light of morning, which makes the buildings, the mining tunnels, the equipment, and the Janissaries' tents look even less real than they do in any case. Only the dogs have woken up and are rambling drowsily through the sand. From the gas station comes the crackling of a defective neon sign that blinks on and off, off and on. A piece of newspaper blows along the sandy main street.

Flinders Range Test Area, Claim 252

Slowly, as if hesitating, the sun rises. Its light reveals an unalterable halt to operations. The Caterpillar stands exactly where we saw it last. In front of it, frozen in confrontation, sit Bandharrawuy and Karrawurra, keeping watch. The surrounding area has come under occupation. Around them more than thirty Aboriginals have bedded down, some of them rolled in blankets like bundles on the ground, others simply lying in the sand, their heads resting on their folded arms and their knees drawn up. Dogs are sleeping among them. We also make out several women. Two metal bedframes, rusty and lacking mattresses, stand in the sand, and each bed has several children sleeping in a heap on the thick mesh. Several tin cans, a Styrofoam cooler, a battered transistor radio, no longer reliable. To judge by the didgeridoo poking out, one of the figures under a patched blanket must be Miliritbi. All these people are freezing in their sleep. A dog lifts its head and yawns.

Coober Pedy

It is late morning, and the place is awake now. Coming from Coober Pedy, a white Land Rover churns its way toward us across the sandy terrain. It passes through the abandoned drive-in theater, whose screen casts a large, angled shadow on the ground. As the Land Rover passes us in a cloud of dust, we see a driver wearing an orange hard hat, next to him a man in a suit, and in the back seat Hackett.

The Land Rover steers toward the Flinders Range Test Area.

Flinders Range Test Area, Claim 252

The Land Rover speeds into the test area and stops just before it reaches the abandoned Caterpillar. The driver, a workman in overalls, immediately jumps out, hurries around the vehicle, and opens the passenger door. Ferguson climbs out, and at almost the same time Hackett. Ferguson, an intelligent-looking man in his midfifties, is wearing a lightweight dark suit and a tie, incongruous in this setting. From his bearing we can tell immediately that he is a man in charge. Confidently he strides straight toward the group of Aboriginals.

Those camped out are all awake now. Without exception they are sitting on the ground, and even the children wear solemn expressions. A small campfire is glowing, and a pot of water placed among the coals is boiling.

Without further ado Ferguson greets the first five Aboriginals with handshakes. Not one of them stands up or says a word.

FERGUSON: Gentlemen. My name is Ferguson, Baldwin Ferguson. I'm the executive vice president of Ayers Mining Company, good morning. May I?

As if it were perfectly normal, he sits down in his suit near the blade of the Caterpillar, facing the Aboriginals, and crosses his legs. It is clear he does not want to tower over the indigenous group. The driver goes back to the Land Rover. Hackett is the only one still standing.

FERGUSON: Hackett, please have a seat. I don't need to introduce you.

Ferguson pulls a pack of cigarettes out of his jacket pocket and offers it to the silent blacks.

FERGUSON: Do you smoke? Please—help yourselves!

The Aboriginals recognize that he respects them up to a point. Miliritbi is the first to take a cigarette, somewhat hesitantly, and then Karrawurra and Bandharrawuy help themselves. Ferguson seems experienced at dealing with such situations. He takes his time, passing around a sleek, elegant gold lighter. Bandharrawuy calmly breaks the filter off his cigarette before he accepts a light.

FERGUSON: I've been told what happened yesterday, but I'd like to hear directly from you what you see as the source of the problem.

The Aboriginals remain silent. Miliritbi turns to Bandharrawuy and says a few words to him in their language.

FERGUSON: Who's your spokesman?

MILIRITBI: We're Riratjingu. Bandharrawuy is our spokesman, he is the keeper of the songs. I am Miliritbi, the eldest elder of the clan. Why were we not asked?

FERGUSON: I'll admit that Ayers didn't initiate any consultation. Please allow me to add that first of all we weren't aware until today of any contact point, that is, of any authorized spokesperson, and second, let me remind you that there didn't appear to be any requirement for consultation, since we are dealing with an area that from a legal standpoint doesn't qualify as a reservation.

Miliritbi confers briefly in whispers with Bandharrawuy.

MILIRITBI: This is a spirit place, a place of dreams. Here the green ants dream. For us Riratjingu and for the Wororas this is a sacred place.

FERGUSON: Please don't accuse us of acting improperly. All of us, you included, are subject to the binding provisions of the Land Rights Act of the Commonwealth of Australia, and we've signed all the required contracts and obtained all necessary permits.

MILIRITBI: This comes under the Rights of the Black Man. What is the Land Rights Act? We've been here forty thousand years longer than you. The green ants will destroy the world if anyone wakes them from their dreams.

FERGUSON: What we're doing here is only temporary. Hackett, explain to them, please, the nature of our operation.

HACKETT: We're just carrying out preliminary tests. We're proceeding on the basis of hunches, because we don't know yet what underground deposits exist.

MILIRITBI: But we know.

Flustered, Hackett pauses for a moment, then he continues.

HACKETT: Maybe I can explain it this way: when you're looking at a tree trunk, you don't what it's like inside, but if you knock on it and then listen, you can tell whether it's hollow. We're listening to what's deep inside the earth here.

MILIRITBI: Don't you see that the green ants have stopped coming to their dreaming place since the digging started here?

FERGUSON: Allow me, with all due respect, to ask a question: am I right to assume that your clan group was originally located in the northern Arnhem Land but was—forgive the term— deported here? So this can't even be considered your traditional clan area? Do you see yourselves as owners of this land?

Miliritbi confers quietly with Bandharrawuy, who now speaks directly to Ferguson for the first time, addressing him with quiet dignity in Riratjingu.

BANDHARRAWUY: (in Riratjingu)

MILIRITBI: He says, We do not own the land, the land owns us. This here is the spirit land of our totem-brother people, and we are its stewards for them. That is what our law commands, from time immemorial. Our totem-brother people have died out, and there is only one living survivor.

He points as he says this to Karrawurra the Mute, who is sitting next to him, his gaze lost in reverie.

MILIRITBI: It is Karrawurra. He is called the Mute. He is a Worora, our brother. Our own spirit land is located farther to the north, but nonetheless the entire Earth is our mother, one great body, and we are a part of it. We shall stay in this place, and you will have to shoot us before you can get us away from here.

FERGUSON: Of course we'll do no such thing. But you must realize that we will take legal steps . . .

MILIRITBI: We have likewise taken steps, of the sort the white man understands. Yesterday we had the Organization of Aboriginal Legal Aid help us prepare a request for an injunction to stop the current tests. We have heard about the court cases in Arnhem Land and in Aurukun in Queensland. We know what we must do.

Ferguson stands up politely.

FERGUSON: Well, gentlemen . . . I will consult with my board of directors.

MILIRITBI: One more thing . . .

FERGUSON: Yes?

MILIRITBI: We have consulted among ourselves. We would prefer to have Mr. Hackett remain in touch with us on behalf of your company, if you agree and he is willing . . .

FERGUSON: That makes sense to me. What do you say, Hackett? It's up to you.

HACKETT: I'm really just a geologist . . .

He is somewhat embarrassed, but at the same time he feels honored by the Aboriginals' trust. He looks at their faces, one at a time, but cannot read them. Then he looks to Ferguson for guidance.

HACKETT: Well, if you think so . . .

Coober Pedy, Entrance to a Mine Tunnel

A fire truck is parked close to the black mouth of a tunnel. Firemen with helmet lamps and powerful flashlights are ready for action. Miss Strehlow is with them, as is Hackett, who has just gone over a detailed map showing the various branches of the tunnel.

MISS STREHLOW: This is where he was seen last.

HACKETT: The problem is that this northern tunnel, see . . . here . . . meets up with a complex of natural caves that we haven't explored completely. It seems to be very complicated and certainly has several levels, but at least the rock is very stable.

FIREMAN: Are we going to need ladders?

HACKETT: I would assume not. The area where you would need ladders is one the dog couldn't have got into.

MISS STREHLOW: My Ben . . . and it's all so dark in there.

Flinders Range Test Area, Claim 252

The area has changed; time must have passed. The Ayers vehicles are gone, but the white trailer that houses the mobile test station still stands where it was. The Caterpillar is parked where it last came to a halt, with the pile of sand and rock still in front of its blade.

Near the blade a proper, if still provisional, Aboriginal camp has sprung up, with small windbreaks made of odds and ends—sheets of corrugated metal, plastic, cardboard. Campfires, bed frames, small piles of trash, beer cans. A number of poles, most of them out of plumb, have been driven into the ground to support a kind of awning consisting of a tarpaulin that tugs at its stakes in the wind and the dust. We see a tangle of dogs caught up in a short-lived scuffle. They vanish completely into a cloud of dust. An older woman throws a rock at them.

Hackett drives up in a Land Rover. With him is Cole, shaking with rage and cursing as he climbs out of the vehicle.

COLE: I told you so! These SOBs . . . these Boongs. Look at the mess we have on our hands now. These skunks . . . all they know how to do is get plastered.

Hackett says nothing. He hands Cole the key to the Caterpillar, and Cole, cursing under his breath, scrambles up to the driver's seat and starts the monster.

HACKETT: So get moving.

Cole angrily shifts the machine into gear, and in a furious, provocative gesture lets it jerk forward about a meter. Hackett remains perfectly calm, knowing that Cole would not dare to defy his instructions and drive any closer to the encampment. Cole works several levers.

COLE: I've got to free up the frigging blade.

A hydraulic arm lifts the blade, but Cole tilts it in such a way that it picks up the entire heap of sand. Next he empties the load into the wind, which instantly shrouds the entire camp and its thirty-some occupants in dust. Cole knew that would happen, and he revels in the mischief. Now he backs up the mighty machine at a speed consistent with his anger, but after about ten meters he brings it to a screeching halt, jumps down, and returns the key to Hackett with a contemptuous expression.

COLE: That should do it.

HACKETT: Thanks. You take the wagon. I can walk later.

Flinders Range Test Area, the Aboriginals' Encampment

Hackett is sitting under the jerry-rigged awning, facing Bandharrawuy, Miliritbi, and Karrawurra. The three Aboriginals are smoking. From the messy camp in the background eyes stare at him unabashedly.

HACKETT: I've been authorized by the company management to make the following offer: Ayers is prepared to put up quite a large sum of money that could pay for a new pumping station for water, as well as buy you a school bus, so the children from all the camps around here can go to school in Coober Pedy.

The Aboriginals remain silent. Bandharrawuy speaks a single word in Riratjingu, and the astonishing fact dawns on Hackett that he most likely understands English.

MILIRITBI: No. He says no.

HACKETT: I'm also authorized to negotiate a certain percentage of the potential proceeds from the operation, but right now those remain undetermined, since we haven't begun to exploit even one mine here. For you that's an area of high uncertainty.

Miliritbi looks at Bandharrawuy. They understand each other without words.

MILIRITBI: No.

HACKETT: Another proposal's been made to put up a building for a center for Aboriginal art, here in Coober Pedy. It would be administered entirely by you. You could preserve your culture there, without outside interference . . .

Hackett is looking increasingly uncomfortable at having to present these proposals. He tries to end the discussion without being rude.

MILIRITBI: No, you don't understand us.

HACKETT: I wish I did understand you, but I come from America, you see . . . Aren't there any white people around here, Europeans maybe, who could help me? My background is so different . . .

MILIRITBI: Yes, there's Arnold, a linguist, but he's not a linguist anymore. He lives out by Andranooka Field with an Aboriginal woman, in an old water tank. And then there's the missionary, a Methodist, but he doesn't have a real function anymore, now that we've taken over the station and run it. He does the book-keeping for us and manages the grocery store.

A pause intervenes; everything has been said. The Aboriginals smoke in silence.

MILIRITBI: Are you a Christian?

HACKETT: No. Or, rather, yes, that's what I was raised as.

MILIRITBI: What would you say if we brought bulldozers and jack-hammers into St. Peter's in Rome and started digging?

Andranooka Field, Water Tank

A desolate former mine. The earth was stripped and then abandoned. It's the most hopeless scene imaginable. A number of wrecked cars lie around, pieces of corrugated metal, rusted railroad tracks, piles of broken glass. A water tank, somewhat dented, lies on its side where it was left when no longer in use. The coat of white paint it once bore has largely flaked off. An opening for a door has been cut with metal shears. Tattered clothes billow on a line in the hot, sandy wind.

Hackett's Land Rover is parked nearby. We see him knock awkwardly and cautiously on the metal tank. A mixed-race child comes out, then another, and another. Then a black woman.

HACKETT: Is Arnold around?

From inside a hoarse voice replies.

ARNOLD'S VOICE: No.

Hackett turns to the woman.

HACKETT: May I speak with him?

ARNOLD'S VOICE: No!

But Hackett persists. A detective's urgency and curiosity have come over him.

HACKETT: It's important. I'm here from Ayers Mining . . .

The voice inside interrupts him brusquely.

ARNOLD'S VOICE: I know that.

HACKETT: I'd like to understand the natives better, and you, Arnold, know more about them than anyone else here.

ARNOLD'S VOICE: I don't know anything. Just one thing . . .

Suddenly Arnold appears in the dark doorway, looking with his white hair and furrowed face like a wrathful deity.

ARNOLD: . . . that you should beat it, go back where you came from. Your civilization destroys everything, and in the end it'll destroy itself.

HACKETT: That's what I heard back when I was in college.

ARNOLD: You know what you look like to me?

He doesn't wait for an answer, instead supplying one himself.

ARNOLD: You look like someone who's on a train that's speeding straight toward an abyss, because up ahead a bridge has collapsed. And even if you were the one person who knew that, the train is moving so fast that all you can do is run toward the back; you can't stop the train or get off. That's all. Goodbye!

The tin door is slammed shut from the inside. It's hung very provisionally on pieces of rusty wire instead of hinges. Several dogs get up from the hollows they've dug in the sand so as to keep cool in the shade of the water tank. They begin to scuffle.

Coober Pedy, Riratjingu Settlement

On the southern outskirts of Coober Pedy lies the housing project some government agency put up for the Aboriginals. With its rows of identical rickety corrugated shacks, laid out as if with a ruler on carelessly poured concrete slabs, it bears a fatal resemblance to a detention camp. Most of the small water tanks are battered or ruptured, doors ripped from their frames lie around, along with broken glass and piles of empty beer cans. Only a few occupants can be seen. Apparently they've all moved out onto the roofed-over concrete slabs, where they squat idly or lie sleeping. The desert floor around them glistens with shards of glass. On the broad area in front of the houses a playground has been set up, a wreck from the day it was dedicated. Rusted metal frames hold chains and rings on which no child has ever done gymnastics and the swing sets' metal poles are half-buried in the sand. An automobile junkyard partially blocks the view of an endless plain full of heat, sand, and clumps of razor-sharp grass.

In the middle of the settlement stands the grocery store, as rundown as everything else. The metal shutter at the entrance is raised, and several men and women are loitering in front or shopping inside. The missionary, in mufti, runs the store. He has a television set and a VCR next to him at the cash register, playing a cassette with one of those sentimental and hypocritical television preachers who have huge followings in the United States. The show is terribly embarrassing and utterly out of place here, but the blacks aren't really paying attention; they are more interested in batteries for their radios and beer. Hackett heads straight for the store.

FITZSIMMONS: Ah, you're from the mining company.

Hackett is grateful for the pleasant reception.

HACKETT: You must be Fitzsimmons. I wanted to meet you. Could I ask . . .

Hackett notices the television and is taken aback. In a flash it becomes clear to him that he can expect no help here. He tries to get out of the embarrassing situation by asking a fake question.

HACKETT: . . . whether . . . whether you sell cigarettes here?

Coober Pedy, Hackett's Place

Like many people who work in Coober Pedy, Hackett lives in a tunnel blasted into sheer rock. The walls are fairly smooth, and in the corner where his bed stands they are covered with printed hangings. The place is furnished simply, with a rather provisional feel. A niche has been set up as a small kitchen with an electric stove and refrigerator. There are empty mineral water bottles on the floor, but everything is quite tidy. Books in a bookcase, family photos on the walls, a table with a typewriter and neat piles of papers.

Hackett is on the telephone, which he pulls behind him on its cord. He lies down on the bed, holding the phone, and stares at the ceiling. He looks depressed.

HACKETT: I'm just not making any headway . . . right, they said no to everything. Nancy, do me a favor and send a telex to Sydney. There's no one in the office now, but tomorrow they'll have it in writing bright and early. The court case? Right, the injunction, I know. What? . . . Really? Against the Commonwealth of Australia, too? Then that must be . . . right, that's what I was thinking, before the Supreme Court . . . yes, yes. . . . Say, Nancy, what are your plans for the rest of the day? Here. At least it's cool in my cave. And you? . . . Oh, I see, with James . . . somewhere. All right, then . . . Depressed? Me? No, no, I have plenty of reading material. Yes, all right, then . . . good night.

Looking disappointed, Hackett puts down the receiver. He pulls a pillow under his head and first looks inquiringly at the ceiling, but it can't tell him anything. Then he runs his hand along the wall hanging, feeling the rock behind it.

HACKETT: Depressed . . . you're depressed. Or is it a toothache?

Coober Pedy, Supermarket

On the wretched main street we see the Coober Pedy super-market, an almost windowless big box. Behind it in the searing sunlight a small, rocky elevation with the typical tunnel entrances. Several cars are parked in front of the store. It is still fairly early in the day.

Inside the supermarket. Nothing sets this supermarket apart from others in the world except that the selection is quite limited. Also, the maintenance is not very good, as we can tell from the cardboard boxes lying around and the broken orange juice bottle on the floor. The juice has already partially dried. Several house-wives with their hair in curlers are pushing their shopping carts listlessly along the aisles.

Hackett, accompanied by Miliritbi, enters through the automatic glass doors. A cashier looks at the two men with suspicion because they go by the line of shopping carts without taking one. The two pass the shelves, paying no attention to the goods. Miliritbi whispers to Hackett.

MILIRITBI: Here's where the children are dreamed.

HACKETT: Pardon? What do you mean?

MILIRITBI: Children are always dreamed by their fathers first, and then they're born. But suddenly the bulldozers came.

The two round the corner of an aisle and come to a halt in respectful silence. They look down the next aisle. A grumpy woman who seems not to have gotten enough sleep overtakes them with her cart and heads down the aisle.

We see what the two men see. Several meters away four Aboriginals are sitting on the floor in the middle of the aisle. They are shabbily dressed and shoeless. The men seem to be in a trance, their eyes half-closed as they hum a monotonous melody. The woman maneuvers her cart past them as if they were not there. She reaches over their heads for a bottle of shampoo, reads the label, puts it back, takes another, and continues on her way. As far as she is concerned the blacks on the floor do not exist.

MILIRITBI: They're sitting where the lone tree stood.

HACKETT: And the management? What do they say?

MILIRITBI: First they threw them out, but the men kept coming back. Now they leave them alone. Look: they've put items on these shelves that not many people buy. Oil paint, shoe polish, things like that.

Elevation near Coober Pedy

Hackett and Miliritbi are sitting atop the highest elevation on the edge of Coober Pedy and gazing into the distance across the dusty desolation of the place. The dusty highway, as straight as if drawn with a ruler, disappears into infinity in the shimmering heat. The two men are engrossed in a quiet conversation that from time to time peters out.

MILIRITBI: We're a part of this land and a part of this rock formation here. We know who made the rivers and where we will be buried someday. We know who the stars are and who resides among them.

HACKETT: And the green ants?

MILIRITBI: They have flown to the east, over the mountains.

He gestures vaguely toward a place far, far away.

MILIRITBI: Years have come and years have gone, and they haven't returned.

They fall silent. A reflective mood comes over the two men; it is obvious that they have developed an understanding.

HACKETT: I wish the world had that kind of clarity for us. I studied rocks and geological formations, and that the earth is round I know, but I have no idea what the universe looks like or where it ends, if it does end . . . You see, if we fire a gun from here, in a mathematical sense, I mean, basically we'll hit ourselves in the back. The bullet would fly around the world and hit us . . .

Miliritbi laughs, the first time we have seen him do so.

HACKETT: They've discovered stars that are fleeing the edges of our universe almost at the speed of light, and I can't rid myself of the feeling that someday someone will be able to show that the universe curves in on itself like the shell of a snail, with only an inside, no outside, and that ultimately these stars are on a collision course with us. There are mathematicians who devote themselves to such questions. See, when a person hangs himself from a branch, he sways on his rope in the wind. How many more ropes would he need in order not to sway, in other words to have his position fixed once and for all in three-dimensional space?

Hackett is on a roll. Miliritbi looks at him, taken aback and somewhat amused.

MILIRITBI: What a question. I don't know.

HACKETT: Well, just one more rope would do the trick. You'd have to tie the rope around his feet and secure it to the ground. Then he wouldn't sway anymore. But that raises another question: how many ropes, or to put it differently, reference points, would we need in the universe in order to stay with absolute certainty in a fixed position? . . . Well, someone came up with sixteen, but that's debatable . . . I hope I'm not boring you, but I find these questions so damned interesting.

Miliritbi smiles but says nothing. He hums to himself, rocking his torso slightly. Then he breaks off and looks Hackett in the eye.

MILIRITBI: You white men and women get lost in your questions. You're lost because you've lost the connection with the land. That's why you're driven but don't know where you're going.

Your presence on this earth will come to an end without meaning, without a goal, a purpose, or a direction.

Coober Pedy, Hackett's Residence

Hackett must have just taken a shower; he is barefoot and wearing only a pair of pants. His hair is still wet. He rubs it dry while
he talks on the telephone.

HACKETT: Hotel reservation? . . . No, Nancy, not for Watson.
　　Did he maybe call you? . . . That worries me; he pokes his
　　nose into everything. No, only the two elders, Miliritbi and
　　Bandharrawuy. . . . How that's spelled? Oh God, I don't know
　　either. . . . I'm bringing the two of them in the Land Rover . . .
　　yes, a double. Tell Ferguson . . . yes, on Monday. Tell Ferguson
　　I'm going to Hepburn Springs for a day; there's a researcher
　　there who works on green ants. I've got to meet him . . . then on
　　Monday I'll be in Melbourne with the other two. Yes, that'll be
　　fine. Take care, and don't talk to strangers.

Landscape near Hepburn Springs

A line of rolling hills, stretching as far as the eye can see. In the
distance, looking delicate through the haze, single trees, also
others bent and battered by the wind. The ground is sandy, and
only now and then do we see spots with sparse clumps of grass.
One feature makes the landscape completely off-putting: here
and there we see gently rounded outcroppings of basalt, poking out of the ground like knobs or lying around like huge balls.
Some of the rocks resemble large petrified human beings, and
onto some of these formations other round rocks have fallen from
above, looking almost like heads. In between we see fallen trees
raising their bleached arms from the sand, and pasture fences
that run up and down the hills in straight lines, with geometric
precision. On the crest of one of the hills, among a number of
these strange, silent figures, at the end of a footpath, stands a
sort of repurposed moving van, from whose open rear liftgate

heavy cables run outside. We can make out a powerful generator inside and various pieces of technical equipment. Next to the truck a tent has been pitched, with a firepit just outside where someone has been cooking, leaving unwashed aluminum pots, pans, and dishes and dirty cutlery lying around. Between two prominent basalt boulders, which seem to have been polished by human hands, we see an odd experimental setup, connected to the cables, which fundamentally consists of a plate with large magnetic coils on each end.

Ernest Fletcher, thin as a rail, almost two meters tall, and very eccentric looking, shows Hackett around. Like British colonial officers, Fletcher is wearing baggy khaki shorts, from which his long, skinny legs protrude. His knees look like knots in a wooden cane. Fletcher is pale and blond, almost albino. His eyelashes are colorless, and his eyes always moist. The strangest thing about him is his speech: he speaks fast, with almost hysterical enthusiasm, and at the oddest places in his explanations he suddenly laughs shrilly for no apparent reason.

FLETCHER: Why here, of all places? Ha ha! Why I'm here? Well, you can't see it, but there's no other place in Australia where the magnetic field's so abnormally distorted. Ha ha ha!

HACKETT: You've measured it?

FLETCHER: Yes, of course. Ha!! And since the green ants are the only known creatures on earth that apparently . . . ha! . . . have a kinesthetic sense for magnetic fields, I confuse them with additional artificial fields. Ha ha! You know what I mean?

HACKETT: I can imagine.

FLETCHER: The military technology folks have already been trying to get in on the action. They think my results will have military applications, like radar, which was based on the way bats orient themselves by sound.

Fletcher picks up a small, flat glass container lying between the magnetic coils and holds it to the light. Inside we see about fifty ants, scrabbling around frantically.

FLETCHER: My little friends here have the ability to change entire landscapes. In one day they can build rock-hard termite
mounds. Ha! Their structures are all constructed in a wedge
form pointing north–south. Ha! You see what I'm driving at.
The green ants eat wood, and they'll eat anything in their way,
even gnawing their way through lead flashings on roofs to get to
the wooden framing. They also dig extensive, branching tunnels
underground. They don't have—ha ha ha!—a complete digestive
system, so they coexist symbiotically with one-celled flagellates
in their guts. From a biological point of view the green ants
aren't really ants at all; they only look like them. They're a kind
of termite, related to cockroaches. So, you get my drift?

HACKETT: And how do you explain the fact that the Aboriginals
are so . . .

He stops in alarm because Fletcher bursts out with a screeching laugh.

FLETCHER: Ha!!! Ha ha ha! The abos! The dark fellas! They must
have observed that before storms our little creatures all line up
pointing north, like metal shavings, like entire armies. Then
they stop in the middle of their running around—that's when
they're dreaming. They're dreaming about the dreamtime,
about the beginning of the world.

Hackett is becoming visibly more helpless and embarrassed.
He takes the glass container with the ants, which are now termi-
nally confused.

HACKETT: I wanted . . . all I wanted, was . . .

But Fletcher is so wound up that he promptly interrupts.

FLETCHER: Ha! The ants are sexless. I hope you know what I mean!
Ha ha! Just once a year they grow wings and fly in gigantic
swarms eastward over the mountains. Only two individuals in
each swarm acquire sex characteristics and mate. The female

becomes the queen, the male the prince consort. You get it? When they return, they drop their wings, build their mound, and organize their crew into workers, warriors, nursemaids, and police to keep order. Then the female lays eggs, often as many as forty thousand in a day, many times her own body weight. The queen becomes immobilized—ha ha ha!—at the very center of the mound. She's fed and grows to a hundred times her original weight and up to two centimeters long. The male . . . ha ha ha! . . . remains small and fertilizes the eggs. Often . . . ha! . . . he takes refuge under the queen, he's easily scared. When the queen—you're following me so far?—becomes infertile, the tribe begins to die off. Warriors come—ha!—in great numbers and lick the queen until she's been licked to death. Ha!!! Ha ha ha ha ha! And then the new generation prepares to fly away.

Hackett is dumbstruck, completely crushed. He does not know what to do with the glass container and finally hands it wordlessly to Fletcher. But Fletcher is so caught up in his flood of explanations that he does not take the container. Eventually Hackett leans it on its side against one of the magnetic coils, but when he notices that the ants are all piled on top of each other, scrabbling helplessly, he carefully lays it down flat.

HACKETT: Thank you very much, Dr. Fletcher . . . actually I wanted to learn something about the green ants, but I think I've learned something about us.

Hackett thinks for a moment, then suddenly begins to laugh uninhibitedly. After a while Fletcher joins in, laughing shrilly.

Melbourne, City Center, Shopping Street

Baldwin Ferguson, impeccably dressed and accompanied by an attractive secretary, holds the door of a large department store in the city to let Bandharrawuy and Miliritbi go out before him. The last one to follow them onto the street is Hackett. He seems very subdued. Both Aboriginals have new clothes, and Miliritbi is wearing a new cowboy hat, but once out on the street he does not know whether to be proud or embarrassed. Despite the new clothes, Bandharrawuy radiates his usual calm dignity. Now he too is wearing an electric watch. It begins to beep softly, Ferguson notices the beeps, takes the watch off Bandharrawuy's wrist, and as they walk along tries to stop the beeping by pressing various buttons.

FERGUSON: I can't seem to make it stop. Hackett, do you have any idea how to turn this thing off?

The group comes to a standstill, and Hackett begins to try the buttons, but he too has no luck.

HACKETT: Do we still have the instructions? I can't figure this out either.

The secretary pulls the case the watch came in out of a plastic bag that contains other purchases. Inside is the instruction booklet.

SECRETARY: Heaven help us—it's all in Japanese.

Melbourne, Busy Street

The group crosses a street with heavy traffic. Miliritbi seems unsure of himself, starting to cross, then stopping, then moving forward again, by which time it is really too late. Bandharrawuy remains perfectly calm. Hackett takes Miliritbi's elbow and steers him across.

FERGUSON: This evening we'll show you the lights of the city from my office. From the thirtieth floor you get a magnificent view. I hope you'll like it.

They continue on their way. Bandharrawuy's watch begins to beep again.

FERGUSON: Even though we're on opposite sides in court, we thought we'd invite you here as our guests so you can get a sense of our side of the story.

Melbourne, Mandalis, a Greek Restaurant

It is evening. Apparently Ferguson has chosen a restaurant that is not too fancy, to make it less intimidating for the two Aboriginals. Simple tables, posters of the Dodecanese Islands on the walls, a newspaper clipping with a photo of Karamanlis upon his return to Athens, Greek music. The same group as before has just finished eating. Mandalis, the proprietor, a small, crafty-looking man, very attractive, brings demitasses of mocha from the kitchen, into which one can see from the dining area. As he approaches the table, he dances a few steps to the Greek music coming from the loudspeakers and sings the words.

In the kitchen the cook, a large, melancholy man who has nothing to do at the moment, begins to dance with his ten-year-old daughter with Down syndrome. He gallantly leads her through a few steps, and the girl chortles with delight.

FERGUSON: The work we do actually benefits all of mankind. What we're digging out of the earth is for everyone; it generates electricity for lighting and heat and cooling, depending on what's needed. Uranium is such a heavy metal that by comparison lead or gold are as light as the cork of this bottle we've just finished.

Hackett drinks his mocha in silence; his cup is too small, however, to hide his face. Suddenly Bandharrawuy begins to sing softly. He beats the rhythm with two spoons. Ferguson leans over to Miliritbi and asks him quietly,

FERGUSON: What's that Bandharrawuy is singing?

MILIRITBI: He's singing a song for the cook because the food was good. He wants to say thank-you.

Bandharrawuy sings, with wonderful good cheer, the respectful song for the cook.

Melbourne, Essendon–North Airport

One of Melbourne's smaller airports, primarily used by smaller private planes. A few older cargo planes are also parked here, obviously the property of several mining companies. In the background a separate section of the airport serves military purposes. Little activity, a clear, sunny morning.

A black limousine is parked next to a private jet. A chauffeur in a gray suit is loading luggage onto the plane. Ferguson and his secretary are being seen off by Hackett, Bandharrawuy, and Miliritbi. Hackett's white Land Rover stands nearby.

FERGUSON: I'll call you from Sydney. Have a safe trip back. You have a long drive ahead of you.

He shakes Hackett's hand and turns to the two Aboriginals, but they have disappeared. We see that they have wandered over to look at an old, big-bellied Hercules transport plane, to which they were magically drawn. Bandharrawuy seems almost mesmerized by the big plane, painted in faded olive green. He seems particularly fascinated by a symbol near the entry hatch that vaguely resembles an ant.

Bandharrawuy begins to whisper to Miliritbi in Riratjingu, pointing at the plane as he does so. Ferguson and Hackett notice what is happening and go over to the cargo plane.

FERGUSON: Gentlemen, I wanted to say goodbye. Is something wrong?

Miliritbi ignores the question. Bandharrawuy whispers to him. Hackett exchanges a look with Ferguson, then takes over the situation.

HACKETT: Sorry, can we help in some way?

At that Bandharrawuy turns directly to Ferguson and speaks to him in Riratjingu.

BANDHARRAWUY: (in Riratjingu)
HACKETT: What's he saying? Does he want something?

Miliritbi hesitates to translate. He looks around at the group. Hackett encourages him.

HACKETT: It's all right. What does he want?
MILIRITBI: He wants the plane.

Great surprise all around.

HACKETT: Really?
FERGUSON: Why?

No answer. Bandharrawuy whispers two or three words.

MILIRITBI: He wants the plane. He wants to have it in Coober Pedy.
HACKETT: But there's no airport.

Ferguson senses an opportunity and jumps in.

FERGUSON: Under some circumstances it would be conceivable
    that you'd get the plane. Except it's not possible in Coober Pedy
    because you'd need a runway.
MILIRITBI: We'll build a runway.

The white men confer briefly in whispers, then Ferguson makes a suggestion.

FERGUSON: It might be good, gentlemen, if you at least witnessed
    what's involved before you make a decision. My pilot could dem-
    onstrate a take-off and landing for you in my plane. Then you
    could see for yourselves. . . . Please give me some time; I'd like

to talk it over with my board first. But under certain conditions, as a quid pro quo, so to speak . . .

MILIRITBI: We Riratjingu will build a runway. In Coober Pedy.

Coober Pedy, Entrance to Hackett's Residence

A regular tunnel entrance in the cliffs, closed off with a door that fits tightly into the opening. Outside a small plaque: Ayers, Seismic Dept., Lance Hackett.

Hackett comes energetically out of the door, carrying a sheaf of papers under his arm. He almost crashes into Miliritbi and Bandharrawuy, who are standing outside.

HACKETT: Good morning.

The two remain silent.

HACKETT: Why didn't you ring? How long have you been standing out here?

MILIRITBI: A short while long.

HACKETT: Ten minutes?

MILIRITBI: Yes.

But Hackett, who has learned in the meantime how to ask questions of the Aboriginals, probes further.

HACKETT: An hour?

MILIRITBI: Yes.

HACKETT: All night? Since last evening?

MILIRITBI: Yes, since last evening. Since sunset.

HACKETT: What's happened?

MILIRITBI: The runway's finished.

Hackett is stunned. He needs time to collect himself, so he straightens his papers.

HACKETT: What? In three days? How is that possible?

Flinders Range Test Area

Right next to the test area on a broad, though slightly rolling plain the runway has been created. About thirty Aboriginals are squatting there, lined up in a row. Hackett drives up in his Land Rover at a high speed, trailing an enormous plume of dust, screeches to a halt, and jumps out. Miliritbi and Bandharrawuy get out somewhat hesitantly. Sure enough: there is a runway, its edges marked with white stones, across the uneven field. But now we realize that it is at most thirty meters long, hardly longer than the cargo plane itself.

HACKETT: For God's sake!

He is really completely surprised.

HACKETT: A plane like the Hercules needs at least six hundred meters, and the runway has to be perfectly flat . . . I'll notify the company; I guess we all failed to take the task seriously enough. I'll make sure the Caterpillars are put to work, but of course you and your men have to help.

MILIRITBI: Yes, we'll help.

Coober Pedy, Entrance to a Mine Tunnel

In the heat of the day a fire truck and a pickup are standing at the entrance to the mine tunnel. Great clouds of dust are swirling.

From the darkness inside the tunnel several lights come dancing toward us. A weary, disgruntled-looking fireman comes out of the tunnel into the harsh light and switches off his flashlight. Then another and another. The search seems to be over.

Elevation near Coober Pedy

Hackett and Miliritbi are sitting on the hill where they sat once before, looking out over the land in the heat. Neither says anything. Miliritbi is calm and cheerful. The sun is slowly going down on the distant horizon.

HACKETT: Another thing. The fire department has ended the search, and Miss Strehlow asked me whether there's a tracker among you, because of her dog.

Miliritbi thinks for a while before answering.

MILIRITBI: We indigenous people don't look for dogs. Dogs find their own way.

A pause ensues.

HACKETT: Will you be coming to work tomorrow with your people?

MILIRITBI: We'll be there.

Near Coober Pedy, Open Field

Broad, almost endless, flat plain, dotted at some distance with the small, whitish cones of tailings from the mines. The Janissaries' tents are veritably innumerable. We see several enormous Caterpillars at work. Mighty clouds of dust are being kicked up. When one of the earthmovers stops, it is immediately shrouded in its own dust cloud, disappearing for a while completely. The operators are wearing orange hard hats and have bandannas tied over their noses and mouths. As we watch, a proper, if provisional, landing strip is being carved out.

Off to one side a camping trailer is parked, serving as a small command post, and next to it several four-wheel-drive vehicles. A sturdy Caterpillar operator storms over to the trailer and pounds on the door, pulling off his bandanna. We recognize Cole, sticky with sweat and dust, and red in the face. Hackett opens the door and stands in the doorway.

COLE: I'm here to complain about the blacks!

HACKETT: What is it this time?

COLE: Most of them ducked out after working for half a day; that's all right, because they're no use anyway. But come and see for yourself what a mess they've made. My Cat stalled out, and what do you think I discovered? Why do you think it won't go?

HACKETT: Haven't a clue.

COLE: During the lunch break those bastards siphoned out the fuel, and now they're all lying around in the bush sniffing the fumes. Those drunks, those no-good SOBs, those . . . oh, fuck it!

Near Coober Pedy

Time has passed. The runway is finished. It is not especially impressive but seems usable. There it lies, waiting expectantly, in the shimmering heat and dust. In the shade of a large sheet of corrugated metal that has been propped up Aboriginals huddle, gazing patiently into the empty sky. Nothing comes into sight there, not a cloud, not a plane. The image fades. We see the sun rising. More corrugated metal has been erected, as well as several temporary shacks. Campfires glow. The blacks are still sitting. We get the impression they have been there for weeks.

The runway, now clearly outlined with white stones, still lies there unused. Above its emptiness resound the strange, deep tones of a didgeridoo.

Coober Pedy, Entrance to a Mine Tunnel

The search has been called off; the entrance yawns like a black hole. Outside the tunnel Miss Strehlow has placed a plastic bowl of dog food. She herself sits motionless on a metal folding chair;

she has put up a light-colored umbrella against the piercing rays of the sun. She too is waiting.

Flinders Range Test Area, Claim 252

A hot, quiet day in the camp that has the field under occupation. The dogs are sleeping. A few Aboriginals stroll about. Nothing is happening. From a transistor radio on the ground blares the voice of a sports announcer; the enthusiasm of the voice booming out of the speaker knows no bounds.

We recognize Watson, asleep in the sand, surrounded by empty beer cans. His head rests on the ankles of Daisy Barunga, herself sound asleep.

Outside Coober Pedy, the Airfield

The Aboriginals continue to wait for the plane. They scan the sky. Suddenly there is a stir. Bandharrawuy stands up. Something appears in the sky.

Yes, it's a plane—a Hercules. It circles over the runway, swooping very low, but then the pilot seems to hesitate. He circles again, calculating the length of the strip. This time the plane lands in a huge cloud of dust and rolls to a stop.

The Aboriginals crowd around the plane. We notice Watson feeling one of the propellers with a knowledgeable air. Several high-ranking functionaries from Ayers disembark and arrange themselves in a sort of row behind Ferguson. Apparently they were planning to hand the plane over in a little ceremony, but with so much pushing and shoving anything organized seems out of the question. Ferguson turns to Miliritbi and hands him an envelope.

FERGUSON: A week from now we'll be facing each other in court, and we hope you will take this as a sign of mutual understanding and mutual respect.

He seizes Miliritbi's hand and shakes it heartily, then he grabs Bandharrawuy's right hand and shakes it like a politician. An employee takes pictures. Only now does Ferguson notice that Hackett is standing among the excited Aboriginals.

FERGUSON: Hackett, come over here! You have to be in the photos, too.

Hackett complies reluctantly. Ferguson keeps shaking the hand of Bandharrawuy, who tolerates it with dignity.

FERGUSON: It is gratifying that you appreciate our willingness to reach a compromise. Establishing the legal status of the project is certainly only part of our common endeavors. Good luck with the Hercules; it's yours now!

But the Aboriginals pay no attention to these declarations. They scramble into the plane, taking possession of it. Moments later they have lit a fire inside. Smoke billows out of all the hatches and doors, as well as out of the open cockpit window. The functionaries from Ayers, still ceremonially lined up, freeze in their positions. Only the pilot is overcome with panic; he forces his way onto the plane.

PILOT: They're setting my Hercules on fire!

But a moment later he reappears, surrounded by clouds of smoke. He seems calmer.

PILOT: It's only a campfire, on the floor inside. I'll drain the gas, just to be safe. Then nothing can go wrong.

The white men find themselves ignored and excluded. Around them swarm women and children, likewise shut out.

Outside Coober Pedy

The scene from farther away. The plane sits there all by itself in the shimmering air, with a bit of smoke eddying out. It appears to be swimming in a silver sea of pure heat. From inside the plane we hear the disconcerting tones of a didgeridoo, a drone pipe.

Melbourne, Supreme Court

The courthouse seen from the outside. It is a massive structure in turn-of-the-century style with an impressive flight of steps leading up to the main entrance. Across the street metal barriers have been erected, and behind them a relatively small but loud demonstration is taking place. Mounted police in safety helmets are patrolling the street. They do not need to intervene; the demonstrators respect the barriers. It is a group of the so-called Urban Aboriginals, carrying banners and shouting in unison, "LAND RIGHTS NOW, LAND RIGHTS NOW!" Some of them are carrying flags, yellow and black with a red circle in the middle. The banners display slogans such as NO URANIUM and LAND RIGHTS FOR ABORIGINALS.

A television crew is there, along with several news photographers.

Courtroom

The courtroom has a high ceiling and wood-paneled walls, but it feels oppressive, like a hall in London's Old Bailey. The arrangement of the witness box, the prosecutor's bench, and the defendant's bench conforms precisely to that of Anglo-Saxon courtrooms. Everything is extraordinarily formal; both the presiding judge and the Crown counsel wear robes and wigs. The bailiff's uniform comes straight from the sixteenth century.

On one side we see Bandharrawuy, Miliritbi, and Karrawurra with a youngish white lawyer, on the opposite side Ferguson, surrounded by a bevy of lawyers and clerks. In the row behind him, Hackett. At right angles to the judge's bench Coulthard, the Crown counsel.

Viewed from the rear of the courtroom: the spectators' seats are packed, with a goodly number of Aboriginals present. Photographers are not allowed in the courtroom, but the press is there. The bailiff enters from a door on the side near the front and pounds the floor with his elaborate ceremonial staff. Everyone in the courtroom rises.

BAILIFF: The High Court is in session, the Honorable Judge Blackwell presiding.

Blackwell, an older gentleman, very intelligent looking, with deep furrows in his face, walks briskly into the courtroom and takes his seat. The rustling of everyone sitting down. Without more ado the judge begins to speak, in a quiet voice.

BLACKWELL: I hereby open the proceeding in the matter of Bandharrawuy et al., plaintiffs, against the Ayers Mining Company Pty. Ltd., defendant, and the Commonwealth of Australia, likewise defendant, represented here by Crown counsel. I consider it important to make clear at the outset that the case the plaintiffs have brought before this Supreme Court is not simply a case like previous ones in which original inhabitants were deprived of and driven out of their traditional lands as a result of the arrival of the white man, which deprivation culminated in the extractive activities of the defendant, the Ayers Company. Although those previous cases will be relevant to this one, we are dealing here with much more consequential questions of extraordinary moral and philosophical import, and we must examine the extraordinarily complex question as to whether the plaintiffs possess a verifiable title, guaranteed by universal rights, to their land valid before 1788, when Governor Phillips by declaration and by raising the flag claimed all the newly discovered land for the Crown . . .

Courtroom, Witness Box

The scene opens with Professor Stanner, a gaunt man, on the witness stand. He is extremely nearsighted and keeps bending so far forward to read his notes that only his shock of gray, tousled hair is visible.

PROFESSOR STANNER: With Your Honor's permission, I shall adopt the classification established by Professor Ernst's study that characterizes the connection between the Riratjingu and Worora clans, and their association with a specific territory that from time immemorial was understood to originate in the so-called time of dreams, as a *mata-mala* combination. At times Professor Ernst even speaks of a *mata-mala* pair. The clan is fundamentally a group that operates according to the principle of patrilineal descent, and every clan is strictly exogamous; in other words, a member of the clan may marry only into the other half of the *mata-mala* combination. This brings us to the concept of the so-called moiety. I must point out that within the discipline of anthropology some aspects of these classifications are disputed, and indeed some aspects remain entirely in the realm of the inexplicable and mysterious.

COULTHARD'S VOICE: Your Honor!

Coulthard, the Crown counsel, has leapt to his feet. He seems agitated.

COULTHARD: Objection! Can you remind the expert witness that it is unacceptable to ramble on this way about the vague and mysterious. With all due respect for Dr. Stanner's qualifications, I must point out that we have to confine ourselves here to verifiable facts.

Blackwell looks up and considers the objection for a moment.

BLACKWELL: Objection overruled. The High Court is capable of reaching its own conclusions. Witness, you may continue . . .

Courtroom, the Gallery

An overview of the rows of spectators. All eyes are riveted on the witness box. It is striking that about a quarter of the spectators, including all the blacks, have risen to their feet and are listening to Bandharrawuy's voice as he speaks with quiet dignity in Riratjingu.

Courtroom, the Witness Stand

Both Bandharrawuy and Miliritbi are standing in the witness box, close together. We have time to listen to Bandharrawuy's strange and lovely language for a while. In the middle of his eloquent statement his watch begins to beep, and without allowing himself to be distracted or even to glance at the watch, he takes it off his wrist and, still speaking, tucks it casually into his pocket. Bandharrawuy concludes his testimony. A pause ensues.

The judge's bench. Blackwell waits to see whether more will follow, then leans forward slightly.

BLACKWELL: Would Clan Elder Miliritbi please assist the court?

In the witness stand Miliritbi now begins to translate:

MILIRITBI: Bandharrawuy, the Keeper of the Songs, has reported the following to the court: "In a past lost in the mists of time the Wandjinas, the spirits, came to this land. They stuck their spears in the ground, and thereupon the hills and the cliffs came into being. Then there came from the east Green Ant Wandjina and dreamt and established his people and built a termite mound. This mound has turned out beautifully, they said to one another, so let us fly east over the mountains. And as they flew, Green Ants Female came to be. Before they flew, they said to one another, Who will guard our mound, who will preserve our place of dreams while we fly? And they said, Let us sing children into existence to guard the dreams, and thus the Wororas came into this world. And when the green ants returned, they discarded their wings and said, Our children have guarded well the place where the dreams reside! Let us give them knowledge of fire, let us give them spears! Innumerable are the years that have passed since then. We belong to the world of songs, where people share everything. And from Ants Wandjina we also have the law that the Wororas and the Riratjingu keep. When it is broken, the green ants will come forth from the ground and destroy the earth." That is what Bandharrawuy has to tell His Honor.

The two Aboriginals remain standing motionless in the witness box until the silence in the courtroom becomes audible.

Melbourne, Supreme Court

It is a gray, rainy day. The courthouse from the outside. Gloomy traffic on the street. The barriers to hold back the demonstrators are still in place, but the space behind them is empty. Nonetheless two mounted policeman are there. They have taken shelter, still on horseback, under a tree. Days must have passed.

Courtroom

An angry confrontation is under way between the Crown counsel, who turns out to be quite combative, and the attorney for the Aboriginals; the presiding judge has to interrupt several times.

COULTHARD: Can the attorney for the plaintiffs please explain to me what this means?

He mimes a vague gesture he has seen a witness make to indicate forward motion.

COULTHARD: In response to a precise question as to where the boundaries of his territory are located, your witness made this gesture. Can you translate that into English for me?

PLAINTIFFS' LAWYER: Your Honor!

BLACKWELL: Order! The Crown counsel will observe proper decorum!

COULTHARD: And when asked about the extent of the clan territory, the witness speaks of "a small long way." What, I should like to know . . .

BLACKWELL: I call upon the Crown counsel to please moderate his tone!

COULTHARD: Excuse me, Your Honor. I just find it upsetting that utterances of this kind by the indigenous witnesses are permitted. And then we heard repeated mention of matters the witnesses had heard about from their forefathers, which fits the definition of hearsay . . .

Blackwell interrupts him and chastises him with such biting precision that we almost receive the impression that the trial is turning in the Aboriginals' favor.

BLACKWELL: I should not have to remind you of the thorough account the plaintiffs' lawyer gave of the precedent established in the case of *Nishaga Indians v. Dominion of Canada* with respect to the admissibility of witness testimony. That question was settled definitively in 1871. As regards your comment about hearsay, let me refer you to the decision in *Angu v. Atta*, argued before the Privy Council of the Gold Coast, 1916. Are you familiar with that decision?

COULTHARD: Unfortunately not, Your Honor.

BLACKWELL: So please be so kind as to familiarize yourself with the case.

He chastises him like a wayward schoolboy.

BLACKWELL: In *Angu v. Atta*, African natives reported to the court with such overwhelming frequency tribal customs that were ultimately grounded only in hearsay that such statements eventually became so notorious that they gained the status of irrefutable truth. The court had to acknowledge this state of affairs and recognize hearsay as evidence. I cannot avoid seeing clear parallels to this proceeding . . .

Courtroom, Witness Stand

Arnold is on the stand. He is wearing baggy but presentable clothing that he must have borrowed from someone. The intensity of the confrontation continues unabated. Arnold veritably hurls his statement at the court.

ARNOLD: Progress! We keep hearing about progress! And where does that leave the Aboriginals? It's progress to nowhere. What have the last two hundred years brought? Extermination, and, when that didn't completely achieve its objective, cultural erasure by white civilization. Simple, garden-variety murder was just one part of it; the rest was done by imported diseases such as measles, smallpox, and syphilis. Parallel to that, on the same monstrous scale, was cultural extermination by means of missionary activities, civilization, domestication, deportation . . .

BLACKWELL'S VOICE: Sir, this High Court is not a forum for political propaganda.

ARNOLD: Your Honor, let me comment on the numbers cited by the original inhabitants that have been called into question here. The Aboriginals' relationship to quantities differs markedly from ours; they do not have abstract concepts of arithmetic. In most of their dialects, therefore, the only numbers for which they have terms are one to three; anything beyond that is "many." If, however, a black cowherd wrangles a herd of six hundred cattle into a corral, he can tell at a glance, without counting, that two cows are missing. Among us that ability is present only in a residual form. If a mother is at the railroad station with her six children, and while she's dealing with the luggage one of the children scoots through the crowd to the taxi stand, the mother will know at a glance, without having to count, that a child is missing . . .

Arnold has calmed down. He pauses, picks up some papers, and for a moment it looks as though he has finished his testimony.

And here, without warning, comes the truly tragic moment of the proceedings. From the plaintiffs' bench Karrawurra rises and makes his way straight to the witness stand. Arnold steps aside, confused. Before anyone can intervene, Karrawurra begins to speak, in Worora.

KARRAWURRA (in Worora):

Not until he has already spoken a few sentences does the judge try to interrupt him.

BLACKWELL: Mr. Karrawurra! You have not been called.
Mr. Miliritbi, please make that clear to Mr. Karrawurra.
MILIRITBI: Your Honor, unfortunately I can't do that.

Karrawurra, who has not understood what is being discussed but obviously recognizes the nature of these proceedings, continues to speak undeterred.

KARRAWURRA (in Worora):

His language sounds beautiful and melodic, softer than Riratjingu. No one interrupts him. After about a minute he finishes and returns with dignity to his seat. Silence in the courtroom.

BLACKWELL: Mr. Miliritbi, the plaintiff Karrawurra was described to me at the beginning of the proceedings as "mute." I'm somewhat confused.
MILIRITBI: Your Honor, that's a mistake. Karrawurra is called "the Mute," but he can speak.
BLACKWELL: Then translate, please.
MILIRITBI: I don't speak Worora.
BLACKWELL: Is there anyone among the plaintiffs or the witnesses who could translate for us?

A moment of silence; no one steps forward.

MILIRITBI: Your Honor, other than him there is no one in the world who speaks his language. He is the only and last one of his people. That is why we call him the Mute One, because he no longer has anyone with whom he could speak.

Silence. We see Blackwell's face. Then Karrawurra's face. Then Bandharrawuy's face. Then Ferguson's face. Then Hackett's face.

Courtroom

And now comes an equally tragic scene. The courtroom is filled to the last seat, as always. The plaintiffs' bench. Bandharrawuy and Miliritbi have risen to their feet. Under his arm Bandharrawuy is holding a longish object wrapped in a wool blanket.

MILIRITBI: Your Honor, I thank the High Court for suspending the trial for two days. We have consulted among ourselves. We have reached a very difficult decision.

BLACKWELL: Please continue.

MILIRITBI: The Riratjingu elders have decided to dig up their *rangga*, which for generations have been hidden in the earth from all eyes. These are our most sacred objects. These pieces of wood and the marks on them explain why we must be on this land, why we belong to this land. We are breaking the deepest secret of our clan. These pieces of wood are not supposed to be seen by anyone; the world could be destroyed as a result of our action. We have decided to show them to the court. We have no choice. But we ask the court to remove the spectators from the courtroom.

BLACKWELL: The request will be honored. Ladies and gentlemen, please leave the courtroom! Mr. Bandharrawuy, is it clear to you that, for reasons having to do with the nature of these proceedings, the defendants as well as a court reporter must be present?

MILIRITBI: Our lawyer has explained this to us.

The courtroom is cleared, the doors closed. All the seats are empty except for those of the parties mentioned, among them Hackett.

BLACKWELL: Please approach.

He turns toward the defendants' section. Trepidation has come over the few remaining participants.

BLACKWELL: Gentlemen, please rise.

Without a word they stand up in a momentary display of respect. Bandharrawuy approaches the bench, singing as with ceremonial gestures he unwraps three longish, flat pieces of wood with ornamental carvings. Miliritbi begins to speak as Bandharrawuy, singing, points to the marks.

MILIRITBI: This. And this here. This is why we must be on this land, why we are part of this Earth.

Blackwell is confused; he does not understand at all. This part is too much for him. Coulthard in his robe and wig bends forward and inspects the sacred pieces of wood with complete incomprehension. Bandharrawuy sings.

Courtroom

Looking down the center aisle from the spectator gallery. The spectators are crowded in together. The trial has come to an end. On the bench the judge has almost finished reading the justification for his decision.

BLACKWELL: For all the reasons I have cited, I must decide for the defendants.

There is stirring in the courtroom, but immediately quiet is restored.

BLACKWELL: The plaintiffs' claims for a radical assignment of rights are hereby rejected; the rights ultimately reside, as before, with the Crown. The ancient inhabitants' motions are inconsistent with the doctrine of Anglo-Saxon Universal Rights, which of necessity had to govern these proceedings. I am deeply grateful to the experts and witnesses for the seriousness and dignity of their efforts. The plaintiffs' motions are hereby denied. The cost of this trial will be borne by the government.

Courtroom, Corridor

The doors to the courtroom are open, and people are flooding into the corridor. A cacophony of voices, photographers snapping pictures, shouts. Hackett has backed Ferguson into a corner.

FERGUSON: This is not the time or the place. What's got into you?

HACKETT: You say that now an out-of-court settlement is possible; what do you have . . .

Hackett is profoundly upset, and only with the greatest difficulty does he manage to preserve appearances. Coulthard in his robe and wig inserts himself between the two men; he looks triumphant. He seizes Ferguson's hand.

COULTHARD: Splendid! Congratulations!

Then he seizes Hackett's hand and shakes it cheerfully.

COULTHARD: Congratulations!

He notices that Hackett is staring at him icily. Coulthard takes a step back. Ferguson tries to adopt a soothing tone.

FERGUSON: You see, Lance, no court in the world can erase two hundred years of history.

At that Hackett explodes, lacing into Ferguson, who is startled by the virulence of his emotion.

HACKETT: Now you're going to have to live with this. Do you have oatmeal for breakfast? How are you sleeping these days? Soundly? Is your swimming pool heated? How are your riding horses?

FERGUSON: Hackett! What's got into you? Whose side are you really on?

Just as abruptly Hackett sinks into grim silence. Flashbulbs going off. Someone shakes his hand.

Airfield outside Coober Pedy

The plane sits brooding in the sun, and Bandharrawuy is alone in the cockpit, staring toward the east. He is dreaming.

Nearby, shaded by a panel of corrugated metal, several men and two or three younger women are sitting around, among them Daisy Barunga. Also there is Watson, the half-breed, who seems to be more than a little drunk. He is trying to impress the women.

WATSON: I'm a pilot. I was the only black pilot in the Air Force. Watson, my captain said, you're something else.

Daisy Barunga giggles. The men, who are used to such talk, pay no attention.

WATSON: I also fixed the engines. I know how to service aircraft engines.

DAISY BARUNGA: I thought all you knew how to do was repair motorbikes.

WATSON: You probably don't believe me, but I'm telling you, I can still give any pilot a run for his money. Watch this!

He feels under pressure to defend his honor. Staggering a bit but completely sure of himself, he makes his way to the Hercules. As he climbs in, he crushes an aluminum beer can with the black swan logo.

WATSON: Dunk a swan before work . . . ha ha.

Seen from outside. He appears in the cockpit, where he begins to fool around with the instruments. On the wing tips lights go on, then off again. Then the rudder in the rear moves. Watson leans out of the cockpit window looking proud of himself.

WATSON: My baby does the hanky panky.

He is obviously continuing to try out the instruments, with which he actually seems to be familiar. Suddenly a loud hum is heard. One of the propellers rotates 180 degrees, then stops moving. Then it turns again, and again. The hum becomes more intense. Suddenly the engine emits a puff of smoke and comes to life. The propeller begins to spin madly, immediately kicking up a large amount of dust behind it. Then the engine is switched off again. The propeller spins to a halt. Watson has made an impression. He leans out of the cockpit window.

WATSON: One tank is still half-full!

He appears in the hatch, proud as a king. The Aboriginals stare at him in silence. Daisy is no longer giggling.

Outside Coober Pedy, Entrance to a Mine Tunnel

Miss Strehlow is sitting on her metal chair under her umbrella, exactly as we saw her earlier. The old lady reacts mechanically, drained of emotion. In front of the dark entrance to the mountain she has placed a fresh bowl of dog food. Hackett is with her. He is unshaven, his clothes rumpled.

Miss Strehlow begins to speak, not addressing anyone. Her voice is completely flat.

MISS STREHLOW: Benny. My dog. My dog is lost. In the dark . . .

HACKETT: Miss Strehlow, here's some iced tea in this thermos. You should take care of yourself.

Miss Strehlow takes the thermos without thanking Hackett and without registering his presence. She looks straight through him into the distance.

MISS STREHLOW: My Ben is gone.

She is beyond tears, out of reach of comfort.

Airfield outside Coober Pedy

Bandharrawuy, Miliritbi, and Hackett are sitting in the cockpit of the Hercules. Hackett has brought sandwiches and Coke and is trying, cautiously, to get something out of them.

HACKETT: I'm curious as to why Bandharrawuy always, and you, too, often sit here in the plane and look toward the east.

Miliritbi hesitates, reluctant to answer, but then he responds after all.

MILIRITBI: Over there . . .

A vague gesture.

MILIRITBI: . . . in the east is his spirit land, where he was dreamed. That's the direction into which the green ants disappeared.

Hackett recognizes that in spite of the great empathy he has developed for the two men he will forever be excluded from the mystery that surrounds the two of them. Hackett pulls out some loose tobacco and rolls a cigarette for Bandharrawuy. He smiles at his own clumsiness.

HACKETT: I've never rolled a cigarette. Here, this tobacco is for you.

The three men sit there quietly and gaze toward the east. Bandharrawuy smokes. We sense that a preliminary stage toward what is called friendship has been negotiated.

Near Coober Pedy, Geological Test Station, Claim 252

Looking utterly confused, two Aboriginals are standing on the edge of the test area. Parts of their provisional camp can still be seen.

The geologists' Land Rovers are back, as are the men in orange hard hats. The scene is abuzz with activity; something is being readied. The radio in Hackett's mobile station is in constant communication with headquarters.

Hackett's station, interior. He is speaking urgently into the microphone.

HACKETT: What? . . . What do you mean, orders from Sydney? I have
 to speak with Ferguson; it's urgent. What, he's not there? . . .
 I must speak with him.

Airfield outside Coober Pedy

Bandharrawuy is sitting in the cockpit and gazing toward the east. Outside in the shade Watson is boasting to Daisy Barunga. Nearby sit a few Aboriginals with their dogs. Heat, swirling dust.

WATSON: I was on the squad's football team. Fullback, right.
 Watson, the squad captain said, you're playing fullback. The
 whole team was made up of pilots. And man, did I ever fly.
 Better than the captain.

DAISY BARUNGA: Really? So you flew?

WATSON: You bet I did. One time when we had an overloaded
 Buffalo, my squadron captain says, You're never going to get this
 plane's ass off the ground. I says, Capt'n, I'm going to light a fire
 under this baby. And man, I gunned her, and that baby's ass
 lifted off.

DAISY BARUNGA: I don't believe you.

WATSON: For real. I'll show you my honorable discharge.

Daisy Barunga giggles. That provokes Watson even more. He has talked himself so deep into imagining himself as a pilot that he has reached the point of no return.

Swaying, with a beer can in his right hand, he stumbles over to the Hercules and scrambles into the cockpit. He takes a seat next to Bandharrawuy, who sees that Watson is obviously drunk but remains serene and calm.

From a distance we see one propeller begin to turn slowly, and then the engine comes on. Dust immediately flies up. But then the next engine comes on, and in quick succession the other two. For some time the plane stands there, just kicking up dust. Then it slowly turns on the sandy runway. It gets under way and picks up speed. We can see that it is zigzagging slightly, and then something happens that one would hardly have thought possible: it lifts off and flies. It takes off oddly tilted, and moments later, in an unpromising curve, it disappears, flying low over a hill and away to the east. Slowly the cloud of dust settles. It leaves behind the empty desert.

Mobile Test Station, Interior

Someone pounds impatiently on the door. Before Hackett can answer, Cole yanks open the door.

COLE: Hackett, you need to come right away. Some of your dark
　　fellows are out here.

Coober Pedy, Early Morning

Coober Pedy lies before us in the pale light like a crater-pocked landscape on a foreign planet that has sought refuge in the unreal.

The sun rises in all its nefarious beauty. Pitiless and indifferent, the desert spreads endlessly before us.

Airfield outside Coober Pedy

A fairly large number of Aboriginals has gathered by the airfield, watching as a search-and-rescue helicopter takes off. Dust and rocks swirl into the air. Another helicopter on the ground is preparing to take off. Four-wheel-drive vehicles, men in orange hard hats, a number of police vehicles. Officers are taking statements. Daisy Barunga is helped out of a rather large armored tactical vehicle by an officer. Then the second helicopter takes off, enveloping everyone on the scene in dust. The airfield, vehicles, people disappear.

Airfield outside Coober Pedy, Armored Tactical Vehicle

Hackett is sitting with two policemen inside the armored tactical vehicle. All three are bending over maps that they have overlaid with a transparency marked with grid lines defining search sectors.

POLICE OFFICER: A-five: negative; A-six: negative; A-seven: negative . . .

HACKETT: But the plane had only enough fuel for forty minutes.

POLICE OFFICER: Yes, I'm mystified too. But see, here in the mountains, with all these gorges. I'm afraid we have to go back and start at A-one again.

HACKETT: Yesterday two Aboriginals from a different clan arrived here from far off in the mountains. I have the feeling they had something important to tell us. But you know these people. They'll sit there all day and not say a word.

POLICE OFFICER: Go see if you can make any headway with these people. Maybe you can get something out of them . . .

Only now do we see how exhausted Hackett is. He clearly has not shaved in three days.

Airfield outside Coober Pedy

Two Aboriginals, clearly from another clan, are sitting in the sand on the edge of the runway, saying not a word. Their faces are turned toward us, their backs to the Coober Pedy Aboriginals. In the background we make out Hackett approaching the two with Miliritbi. Both men are wearing ragged shorts. They are barefoot and shirtless. One of them has painted his face with ochre. Each is holding several spears.

Miliritbi and Hackett have now reached the two men.

MILIRITBI: They talked earlier. You should hear it for yourself.

Hackett squats down beside the two. A period of silence follows. Then the older of the two men begins to sing briefly in his dialect. Miliritbi translates.

MILIRITBI: You have heard of the Great Winged Ant. In springtime
the ants cast off their wings. In the east, in the Oodnadatta
Gorge, they have found a wing.

From a great distance we see the Aboriginals squatting together and looking eastward; they begin to sing. We recognize Hackett among them. The image remains in place for a long time. The desert is vast. The desert is empty.

Andranooka Field, Water Tank

Carrying a bundle of bedding on his shoulder, a barefoot Hackett stands before Arnold's old water tank. He knocks. Arnold appears.

ARNOLD: Any news of the plane?

HACKETT: Yes, it's been found. Near Oodnadatta . . . Actually I'm
here for another reason. I wanted to ask if there isn't another
water tank like this one around here.

Near Coober Pedy, Flinders Range Test Area, Claim 252

With a loud crack a detonation goes off, then a series of explosions at intervals of at most a second, as if drawn along a string. The detonations march straight toward the small, rocky elevation, and there the last explosion in the series takes place, at the very spot where the green ants dream.

The Little End of the World

The last detonation crumbles in slow motion, the images crack and crumble. We see torn-up ground, bare trees on the ground with thousands of beer cans lying around them. We see drunk Aboriginals in a foreign city. Remains of Caterpillars. Automobile wrecks. The camera wanders aimlessly through a wretched Aboriginal encampment. Dogs, garbage, filth. A shot of white suburbs. Then the camera circles for a rather long time around a single aluminum beer can. It has a black swan on its side.

Far-flung Land

A title appears:

A TORNADO TOUCHED DOWN THAT CAUSED CONSIDERABLE DAMAGE IN THE NORTH. IN THE NAMING OF THESE STORMS THE LETTER T HAD BEEN REACHED. THE METEOROLOGISTS NAMED THIS ONE TRACY.

An incredibly immense land with the darkest, blackest clouds overhead. We see the twister. From the blackness of the clouds a curving, terrible-looking tube has come down to the ground and moves across the land, like the trunk of a fearsome animal. The uncanny sound of a drone pipe echoes far and wide. For a long, long time we see the terrible trunk of the tornado, sucking everything in its path into the clouds.

Cobra Verde

———

AUTHOR'S NOTE

This film narrative is based very loosely on motifs from a novel by Bruce Chatwin, *The Viceroy of Ouidah,* published in 1980 by Jonathan Cape (London). Anna Kamp's German translation was published by Rowohlt (Hamburg) in 1982 as *Der Vizekönig von Quidahl.* I thank Mr. Chatwin for allowing me to quote verbatim a few passages from his book.

CHARACTERS

Francisco Manoel da Silva	*aka Cobra Verde*
Zé Piranha, Manuelzinho	*gold diggers*
Lucia	*a mulatto woman*
Don Octavio Coutinho	*plantation owner, colonel*
Doña Epiphania	*his wife*
Bonita, Valkyria, and Wandeleide	*his daughters*
Euclides	*nine-year-old boy*
The yovogan	*minister of the king*
Barnabo	*missionary*
Taparica	*drum major*
Bossa Ahadee	*king of Dahomey*
Kankpé	*the king's brother*

Bakoko   *Kankpé's confidant*

Plantation owners, pilgrims, gold diggers, slaves, Amazons, fetish priests, dancers, ship captains, rowers, and many others

Caruaru, Street

The murderous light, glaring, searing; the heavens birdless; dogs lie dazed by the heat. Demented from anger, metallic insects sting glowing stones.

Ahead of us a bumpy cobblestone street makes its way uphill, with Caruaru's small whitewashed houses on either side. Higher up the town peters out amid the leafless brush of the Sertão. There in the dust, the withered brambles, and scree, the heat has taken up permanent residence, cruel, undisguised, and shimmering.

Facing us, an old man sits on a stool in the middle of the street. He is one of those itinerant minstrels and poets often encountered on market squares in northeastern Brazil. When he plays his fiddle, which he made himself from plywood, he clenches it far back, almost in the nape of his neck. His face is gaunt, furrowed with age. His eyes have seen everything, and his mouth reveals how greatly he must have suffered. Only a few of his teeth are left. Handsome old hands, somewhat knotted. On his head he wears a battered straw hat.

"That'll cost you," the man says, looking us in the eye. "Ladies and gentlemen," he continues, "you'll have to pay if you want me to sing the ballad of Francisco Manoel."

We hear the clink of a few coins. "Thank you," the man says. "You will now hear the ballad of Francisco Manoel da Silva, the poorest of the poor, the bandit Cobra Verde, the ruler over the slaves. He became a viceroy in far-off Africa. He was the alonest of the alone."

With a stiff gesture he picks up his fiddle. His eyes travel to the distant horizon, his voice is hoarse and creaky with age.

> *Francisco Manoel's mother sighs,*
> *Francisco, I feel only aches and dread.*

Francisco Manoel's mother cries,
Francisco, leave me. I will soon be dead.

Eleven years of drought, the rocks are sick.
The world is dying. Evil is a trick.

I will die now. Be quiet, or the bench will crack
From sadness. Do not move. Stay still.
The water, the earth and the sun turn black.
God, in His Perplexity, pretends it's His Will.

Francisco, traveling, reads a line in the sky.
"Don't set your eyes on the salt sea shore.
Don't reason. Don't argue. Don't ask us why.
Fate will send you a lover, and one friend more."

The Sertão

A small, utterly wretched hut, lost in the lostest of all wastelands, the Sertão. A freshly dug grave with a cross fashioned from two dried branches, and kneeling before it Francisco Manoel, hat in hand. "I should keep still in the face of this land, she said." He murmurs to himself, letting his eyes roam over the boundless solitude. He stands up. He tosses the fleshy branch of a cactus into the fire and burns off the thorns. Then he drops it in front of the emaciated cow, who has been standing there all the while, the light gone from her eyes. Nearby the skeletons of an entire herd that perished of thirst. Francisco Manoel looks down at the grave. "Her oases were not of this world," he says. "'Be still in the presence of the cow,' she said, 'she is the last. Loud talk will kill her.'"

Francisco Manoel takes a step that places him directly in front of the cow, who seems not to register him anymore. Without warning he bellows at her from very close, directly into her face. "Eat that," he shouts at her. "I eat it, too." The cow merely sighs deeply. Then she falls down dead.

Monte Santo

Above the Sertão, this endless world of endless drought and endless poverty, rises a mountain range with a sharp ridgeline to which a footpath ascends in serpentines, worn into the jagged, pale quartz. Once at the top, the path follows the ridgeline to a whitewashed chapel, where it ends. Shabbily clothed pilgrims form an unbroken line as they toil up the mountainside on their knees. Farther up the jagged rock is discolored from traces of blood left by scraped knees.

Profound, ecstatic emotion, prayers murmured soundlessly, and some of the pilgrims flagellate themselves with leather straps studded with nails.

Seen from above, the procession of misery shrinks to a thread of human figures strung across the landscape. An entire people, all the misery in the world, disappears from view beyond the horizon.

Amid the throng of pilgrims we recognize Francisco Manoel, painfully making his way on his lacerated knees up the Via Sacra. His eyes are glowing. Years of drought have twisted his mouth into an expression of rage.

Upon reaching one of the last stations of the Cross, he suddenly pauses. Here a loose pile has been created of human limbs fashioned out of wood and other votive items, and among them what is left of spent fireworks. He pauses because something terrible is taking place inside him. He picks up the remnants of a rocket and inspects it without really seeing it, mechanically, absent-mindedly. Then, suddenly, almost with a jolt, his facial features take on a look that will not change from now on.

Francisco Manoel stands up, steps out of the line of pilgrims, and peels his pants off his bloody knees. A haggard young priest with a dark, ecstatic gaze and dark hairs on his fingers hurries over to him. "My son," he says, "there is only one station left." "The Sertão will kill us all," Francisco Manoel replies.

The priest recoils upon encountering this defector. "The blessed Virgin," he says, "weeps bloody tears today on Good Friday for all those burdened with care." "Priest," says Francisco Manoel, "take these wooden limbs here, pile them up high, and wait until the Virgin places something to eat on them, then light a fire, and I will come."

The priest, horrified, makes the sign of the Cross. Francisco Manoel turns away abruptly. "I am going; I must get away from poverty if it costs me my life. I am leaving this life," he says, and starts down the mountain, his knees stiff from being bent so long.

Serra Pelada

Dusty earth, red as if drenched with the blood of a people. A primitive hut, hastily slapped together; in two hammocks sleep men so dead tired that it seems they might never get up again. A trickle of reddish water, cloudy with clay, is channeled into a simple setup for washing gold. A ragged, scrawny man slowly shovels dusty red earth into a wooden drum through which the water runs. The water then flows down a slanted ramp fashioned from boards, passing over narrow slats, and flows away, sluggish and dirty. The man pauses, waits until all the water is gone, then inspects the boards and with a small scraper carefully collects tiny particles of gold dust.

A man who wears his trousers rolled up to his knees appears, his back bent under a heavy sack filled with sand.

His clothing is in tatters and red from the dirt, his hair red, his skin, his face, his bare feet. Exertion, heat, and sweat have left their traces in the skin of his face, which is so disfigured that not until we hear his voice do we realize that this is Francisco Manoel. He empties the sack onto a pile. "How is it looking today?" he asks. "Today we may get half an ounce," the man says, "a little better than yesterday."

Francisco Manoel wipes the back of his hand on his pants, then runs it over his face. "What do you mean by *we*?" he asks irritably, glancing at the men asleep. "When are Manuelzinho and Zé Piranha getting back to work?"

"That's none of your business," the other man says. "The claim belongs to them. Just be glad we're letting you work with us."

Francisco Manoel tosses the empty sack over his shoulder and leaves; we follow him. And now we see that the shack, the trickle of water, and the gold-washing setup are not alone; the entire landscape is dotted with such trickles, and thousands of men are engaged in the same work. Our view widens out, and we realize, to our surprise, that an enormous valley high in the mountains is filled to the rim with such activity.

And then this: Francisco Manoel makes his way to an escarpment, where the land falls off abruptly. A huge crater, created by human beings, opens up before us, in which, as in a gigantic ant heap, tens of thousands of men are doing the same thing simultaneously, with their bare hands. The construction sites for the Egyptian pyramids must have looked like this, the difference being that here the work reaches far down into the ground. The entire vast swarm of people is uniform in color: they are all covered in reddish dust and clay. At the bottom of the pit, at a depth of almost a hundred meters, and on its steep slopes, men are digging into the earth, most of them with their bare hands and only a few with picks and shovels, filling sacks, and hauling them in endless processions up serpentine paths to the rim of the immense hole. Others climb hundreds of rickety ladders to get up and down the slopes. From time to time small landslides occur, avalanches of dust let go and for a while shroud everything that moves. It is incredible drudgery in the quivering heat. Dust, sweat, panting; the men are so exhausted that they hardly speak. Under the heavy sacks the men move forward only in a sort of trot, lest they collapse under the weight. Eighty thousand men labor here on the brink of exhaustion, half-staggering, half-driven by lust for gold. It is pure slavery, albeit voluntary.

Francisco Manoel disappears in the almost unbelievable crush.

Gold Smelting

The gold is smelted in a wooden shack open on one side. About thirty charcoal fires are kept white hot with bellows. A rough board fence, guarded by heavily armed men who would have no hesitation about committing murder, keeps the curious crowds, lured by the gold, at a distance. Feverish, haggard faces, glowing eyes, silent mouths. They watch, transfixed, as the gold dust is smelted.

The smelted, furiously seething gold is poured into hollow ceramic squares, where it cools, smoking and hissing. Clumps the size of a man's fist congeal and are seized with tongs by smiths who hammer them into shapes with smooth edges.

Between the smiths' feet, crouching and crawling on the ground, a grossly deformed boy, to whom one of the smiths tosses a pail half-full of trash and slag. In the slag bits of gold can still be found. The boy scuttles away like a crab, dragging the pail behind him and uttering inarticulate sounds.

Right beside the smithy stands an equally dilapidated wooden shack, the government bank, which buys the gold. The armed men escort the smelters to sleazy, sweaty bank employees; apparently the smelters are forced to sell their product here, and apparently the purchase price set by the government is quite low. Filled with distrust and dissatisfaction, the men curse under their breath. It also looks as though the scales are rigged.

Among those waiting outside, squeezed in shoulder to shoulder with the other men and breathing in their acrid sweat, we see Francisco Manoel. When his three partners emerge from the bank, he has to fight his way through to them because they avoid meeting his eyes. "Where's my share?" he demands bluntly. "There was none this time," says Zé Piranha, a man with a brutal face and sleepy eyes. "The bank kept it," adds his partner Manuelzinho, making no effort to sugarcoat the lie. The third man involved in the gold washing musters another explanation: "The license for the claim has to be paid off first, and besides you've been living and eating with us. Once you've worked half a year for us, there'll certainly be a share for you."

Without warning and without a sound Francisco Manoel attacks Zé Piranha, the one standing closest to him. After a brief scuffle Francisco Manoel is knocked to the ground. As he lies there, the others kick him savagely. None of the others nearby finds the incident at all abnormal.

Serra Pelada, Shack, Night

Three hammocks, sagging with the weight of the men sleeping in them, can be seen in the dim moonlight, bright enough for us to see that two of the men are holding guns. From the Sertão, strange, furious insects bawl a concert into the night. Even breaths and snores from one of the men.

From the post to which it is attached at its foot end, a vibration goes through one of the hammocks. With a powerful thrust a machete has plunged into the wood, singing as it whizzed through the air. Zé Piranha, instantly wide away, clutches his gun. The huge, dark figure of Francisco Manoel looms over him, a machete in his hand. "I want you to be awake when you die," he says, then slays him with a single, terrible blow. At once the other two wake up. Still partly asleep, Manuelzinho fires a shot into the air. Wielding the machete over his left shoulder, Francisco Manoel strikes Manuelzinho, and without a sound flees into the darkness. Shouts, people pursuing him, and long after he has disappeared shots continue to ring out. A fiddle joins in the din, then comes the voice of the singer.

> *Eleven years' poverty, no gold, only sweat*
> *The sun makes him blind, the heat makes him wet.*
>
> *Francisco continues on, in the heavens above:*
> *A sign to heed: beware of the sea.*
> *Fate will give you a woman to love*
> *And a friend to hold fast in a world that's empty.*

The Woman to Love

Along a dusty road through the Sertão, black slaves carry a sedan chair with damask curtains. A servant walks ahead, carrying a parasol such as aristocratic ladies used in the Rococo period when they played at being shepherdesses. The scene reveals that the occupant of the sedan chair must be a lady of distinction. Spirited greyhounds bound around the little procession. They dash into a clump of brush, barking ferociously, and flush out a man wearing a broad-brimmed leather hat and bandoliers across his chest. Over his shoulders is draped a tattered silk poncho that must once have been green. It flutters in the breeze. He is barefoot. He fires a shot. We recognize Francisco Manoel, the bandit.

The black slaves promptly set down the sedan chair and with shrill cries flee into the thorny bushes, with the greyhounds baying behind them. With splendid serenity an incredibly beautiful young mulatto parts the curtains of the sedan chair and steps out. She is wearing fine jewelry, a seductive dress of white lace, and delicate shoes on her tiny feet. Francisco Manoel points his gun at her and fires a shot just over her head, causing twigs to fall from a branch behind her. "Your money or your life," says Francisco Manoel.

The beautiful woman is not impressed in the slightest. In a remarkable, wonderfully flexible dance-like motion she glides toward him, her arms and torso moving to the rhythm. Once face to face with him, she spins to show him her back, then bends her upper body all the way back until her head is looking at him upside down. "My life," she says and offers him her mouth to kiss.

Francisco Manoel tosses his gun aside, laughs, and kisses her.

Campfire

Surrounded by dusty bushes on the nocturnal Sertão, the beautiful woman and Francisco Manoel are making love by the flickering light of the fire. Both of them pause at the same moment, as if by previous agreement, and begin to laugh. They roll with laughter in the sand and kiss each other. Then, at the same moment, they suddenly go back to their lovemaking.

Toward morning the beautiful woman awakes in the arms of Francisco Manoel, who has been lying there quietly, wide awake. "What's your name?" he asks her. "Lucia," the woman says. "I belong to the household of Don Virgulino. I'm his favorite." "I'm the bandit Cobra Verde," says Francisco Manoel politely. As if on cue, the laughing and rolling around resumes.

Only now does the beautiful woman seem to notice that Francisco Manoel's hands are so studded with gold rings that they are completely stiff. She looks at him, then without a word pulls off her pretty gold ring and places it on his little finger, where she finds a little gap. Francisco Manoel is moved and gentle and proud. "Why don't you have a horse?" she asks him. "There's no horse I trust," Francisco Manoel replies. "Every day you walk forty miles through the thorns; why are you barefoot?" she continues. "There are no shoes I trust," Francisco Manoel tells her. "There are no people I trust, either," he says, "but I love you." They look at each other and remain silent. A small wind gust rolls the parasol away from the campsite.

Lençóis

Looking as if it has been baked by the heat, the town of Lençóis sits in the middle of the Sertão with sparsely vegetated hills all around, and an almost dried-up river coming from the mountains. Only in a few hollows in the red, brittle rock has some water pooled. Bumpy pavement, squat, whitewashed houses, in between a few grand buildings with small arcades in the colonial style. Trade in diamonds gave this village, which otherwise would have perished, a touch of grandeur. A church on whose ledges withered clumps of grass and cacti have taken root, a few bars that have seen better days, a handful of sleepy shops. A horse is gnawing at the post to which it is tethered. Where the town widens to accommodate a small square, we see a few people scooting into their houses.

Now dark lizards with orange heads also flee into gaps in the walls. A man strides slowly down the street, his gun in his arm, his eyes darting about, full of mistrust. Doors close, window shutters are pulled to, and we hear locks being bolted; whispering, fear. Slowly the man enters the square. Behind their doors, the townspeople hold their breath. The man slowly turns in a circle. It is Francisco Manoel, the bandit Cobra Verde, covered in dust, his lips dry and cracked, his feet bare. The dangerousness he projects spreads unmistakably around him.

A single bar, half-shaded by the arcades, remains open, so open that it almost seems like a trap. Very warily Francisco Manoel enters the room and looks around for a place to sit. From behind the bar comes a boy of about nine, his torso misshapen like a short tree trunk. His head seems to rest between his shoulders. His face looks very young and very old at the same time, his eyes sorrowful and clever.

"The gun stays outside," says the boy. Francisco Manoel gives him a surprised look; no one has ever spoken to him this way. "I mean it," says the boy; "otherwise you won't be served." Francisco Manoel goes slowly back to the door and leans his gun against the frame. "I want something to eat," he says. "Tell your father Cobra Verde is here." "I have no parents," says the boy. "This is my bar, and I'm not afraid of you." Francisco Manoel sits down with a smile. "My name is Francisco Manoel," he says. "And my name is Euclides," the boy says, "Euclides Alves da Silva Pernambucano Wanderley."

Francisco Manoel extends his hand to him. "I'm also a da Silva. With your hunchback you're the only upright man here."

Now it is the boy who shows surprise; no one has ever said that to him. He looks down at himself. "It's only my chest and shoulders," he says.

"I've carried whole mountains on mine," says Francisco Manoel. "My friend, bring me something to eat."

Lençóis, Bar, Night

A kerosene lamp lights half of the bar where Francisco Manoel and his friend Euclides are sitting at a table drinking sugarcane brandy. In the village outside no one is stirring. Only the cicadas on the Sertão saw away at the night. The two are having a confidential conversation, their heads close together. The boy has talked himself into a state of excitement; his ears are aglow. Both have fallen silent for a moment.

"And how do you know all this?" Francisco Manoel asks. "From our priest," says the boy, "and he learned it from the bishop." "And where is there snow?" asks Francisco Manoel. "You can see it from here," says the boy and leads him to the open door.

Outside the moon appears very large in the sky, and both of them look up at it. "There's always snow on the moon," says the boy; "that's why it's so white. It's cold on the moon."

Back inside, at the table lit by the kerosene lamp. "And here on Earth?" Francisco Manoel asks. "That's far away," says the boy, "far, far to the west, four years on a horse and ten years on foot. Then come mountains, which get higher and higher till they're above the clouds. And up above the clouds, that's where you find snow. It falls only at night, like feathers, but only above the clouds. Then everything becomes all white and soft. The animals' coats get white, the snow lions, the rabbits, even the eagles get white plumage. When you walk through the snow your feet are very light, and the flakes fly apart like feathers. When you're thirsty, you warm snow under your arm, and it flows like water. But it tastes a little salty." "Where does that come from?" Francisco Manoel asks. "The moon," the boy explains, "sucks salt out of the sea and at night the mountain peaks draw the flakes down. It's only as much salt as in our tears. Maybe the snow is made entirely from tears."

The two look at each other in silence for a long time. Then they both drink at once. Winged insects sizzle as they fly through the flame of the lamp. "In a couple of years," the boy says, "I'm selling the bar, and then I'll take a horse and go west, to the mountains."

"I'm going east, to the sea," Francisco Manoel says. "The Sertão dries out people's hearts and kills the livestock."

"You have to watch out for the sea," says the boy; "it's the cradle of storms, and it's the cradle of snow. I heard that from the priest."

Lençóis, Cemetery

On the edge of Lençóis, where the red cliffs rise in steps, the cemetery is located on a small plateau. At first it does not look like a cemetery at all but like a snow-white, mysterious city, like something in a dream. Every tombstone looks like a little cathedral, a little heavenly palace in Byzantine style, with domes, arches, small towers, and carvings, all chalky white, an imaginary heavenly Jerusalem. The heat flickers against the surrounding cliffs and adds to the graveyard's unearthly appearance.

Francesco Manoel and the boy are standing there looking at it. "That's how the heavenly Jerusalem looks," the boy says. "You're going east now to the sea, and I'm going west to the mountains, and if you go even farther, across the sea, and on the other side I continue beyond the mountains, we will meet again. That is on the other side of the world, in Africa. Jerusalem is in the mountains, on the northern edge of Africa. It's located so high up that it snows there. If you see a city that looks like this one, you'll be in Jerusalem."

Francisco Manoel shakes his hand. "I've never had a friend before," he says. "Farewell."

The Ocean

A broad bay, white sand, palm trees, an incomparable beach. Francisco Manoel is seeing the ocean for the first time. He must have been standing here for quite a while, for busy little crabs are scurrying back and forth around him, engaged in inscrutable tasks. When they pick up speed, they stand up higher on their little legs, and their tempo changes suddenly. When Francisco Manoel raises a bare foot, suddenly all the crabs pause in the middle of their running about, and when he stamps on the sandy ground, they disappear in a flash into their holes.

Beneath three lone palm trees is a small bar with simple stools, a counter, a shelf with bottles, and a roof of woven palm fronds. The proprietor is asleep, his head on the counter. Nearby, black slaves are hacking open coconuts with machetes under the watchful eye of a white overseer, while a slave hovers behind him holding a sunshade.

Francisco Manoel enters the bar. He lays his gun on the counter, which wakes the proprietor. "A bottle," says Francisco Manoel. "Five cruzeiros," says the owner. "I have no money," says Francisco Manoel, but he pulls a gold ring off one finger. Astonished, the proprietor places four additional bottles on the counter for him. "I need only one," says Francisco Manoel and sweeps the bottles off the counter. They fall to the floor and smash. He uncorks the one remaining bottle and pours the brandy into the sand. Then he crosses the beach and wades into the ocean. When the water is almost to his chest, he stops and fills his bottle, quietly and seriously, as if it were a sacred ritual. He tastes the water by licking his fingers.

Back at the counter he lets the water drip from his clothes. He carefully corks the bottle. "Do you want to carry the ocean around with you?" the proprietor asks rather stupidly. "Have you ever heard what snow is?" Francisco Manoel asks in return.

The Beach by Night

The moon has risen large and full above the tranquil ocean. Francisco Manoel is leaning against a palm tree. Nearby drums are pounding, interrupted now and then by the strange sound of the single-stringed berimbau. Black slaves have gathered on the beach and are dancing capoeira, a wild form of movement in which the dancers whirl, kick, butt heads, and turn somersaults in simulated fights. The apparent tangle of bodies is in reality the perfected execution of a complicated series of movements.

Francisco Manoel looks on in astonishment. Near him stands a young black man in white linen pants, his naked torso beaded with sweat. The dancers whirl faster and faster, their bodies crisscrossing in intricate patterns, until the first tumble to the ground in ecstasy, as if struck by an ax. "What's wrong with them?" Francisco Manoel asks. "That was Exu, the messenger," the black man replies. "He struck them between the shoulder blades."

An older man steps between the drummers and begins, speaking in a strange African language, to utter repeated invocations in the direction of the open sea. With a rod he touches the roots of a large tree.

"That's the loco tree," the young black man explains to Francisco Manoel. "Its roots wend their way under the ocean all the way to Itu-Aiyé in Africa, to the homeland of the gods. He is calling on our ancestors." "What's Africa like?" asks Francisco Manoel. "In Africa there are great royal palaces built of mud," the young man says. "They are plastered with skulls and their roofs are decorated with skulls. There are peoples who exchange gold dust for tobacco. There is a sacred serpent that a long, long time ago was a rainbow, and there is a king with testicles as large as avocados. His kingdom is located on the gulf of Benin, and the country is called Dahomey."

Francisco Manoel looks out over the night-dark sea. From his gaze we can tell that the name *Dahomey* has taken root in his imagination.

Bahia, Pelourinho

Pelourinho Square in Salvador de Bahia, the Square of the Pillory. Here slaves are whipped in public. The triangular square extends up a hill. Smooth pavement, an ornate Baroque church on the left, all around opulent colonial houses with splendid balconies from which, as from the carved windowsills, luxuriant vines and ferns cascade. Everywhere ornate cages with colorful tropical birds. The houses painted in a great variety of colors, decorated with a lavish tropical sense of style.

At the lower end of the square, where the triangle comes to a sharp point, an inquisitive crowd has gathered around the pillory. Behind it the city of Bahia, with its colonial buildings and Baroque churches, stretches up and down the hill. Half the buildings seem to be churches; on some hill crests churches are arrayed side by side. Slender palm trees tower between them into the sky, which is filled with the cries of swallows.

We see Francisco Manoel among the curious. Most of those in the crowd around him are black slaves. At a certain distance white gentlemen observe the scene from their sedan chairs. A slave is being brutally flogged. He has been placed with his face to the pillory, and his hands have been tied to it so high up that he can barely touch the ground with his feet. His shirt has been torn off. Beating him mercilessly on his back, already bloody, is another slave, who has apparently been given privileges as a reward. The victim does not cry out; he only groans very quietly. Two other victims, however, lying under guard on their stomachs and hiding their faces under their arms, are wailing loudly. Their turn has not come yet. The black spectators stand there in silence, pure fear in their faces.

Suddenly one of the two lying on the ground jumps up and in utter panic tries to escape, knocking over two spectators in the process. As if he has run into a wall, he bounces back upon encountering Francisco Manoel's stare, which radiates implacable power. "Stay where you are," he says; "otherwise it will go much worse for you." The slave is promptly seized by three men. "Let him go," Francisco Manoel admonishes them; "he will go to the pillory of his own accord." The slave goes to the pillory. "Don't tie him," Francisco Manoel says; "he will stay there of his own accord. What is your name?" he asks the slave. "Jair," the man replies, while the first blows of the whip are already striking him. Without being tied, he stands there and takes them.

A corpulent man in his late fifties extracts himself with some difficulty from one of the sedan chairs. He pushes his way purposefully to the site of the action. "Hey there, Barefoot," he says, "what's your name?"

"Da Silva," says Francisco Manoel, "Francisco Manoel da Silva."

"I am Colonel Octavio Coutinho," the man tells him.

We see Francisco Manoel size him up. The colonel is a magnificent wreck. A slave from his retinue has rushed to him in the meantime and is fanning him with an ostrich feather to give him air. The two men, different though they are, seem to take a liking to each other.

"I need someone like you," the colonel says. "I have six hundred slaves working my fields, and my overseer is useless. I'm the king of sugar."

Manor House

A grand, generously proportioned room. Crystal chandeliers, brocade draperies, a parquet floor, furniture worthy of a princely residence. Everything overly ornate in the best tropical Baroque style.

Luxuriant houseplants, a gilded cage with a brilliantly colored parrot. The colonel is lying on a sofa in a silk dressing gown while a pretty black slave fans him. By the table where a small stack of new undergarments has been placed, Doña Epiphania, the lady of the house, her face sour, parchment-colored, full of unbending religiosity. In the door to the salon the three daughters, Bonita, Valkyria, and Wandeleide, are giggling over the newly arrived Francisco Manoel but pretending their amusement is focused on the little marmoset to whom they are feeding fruit.

Francisco Manoel has parted his hair and tamed his wild locks with pomade; his boots seem to be at war with his feet, and in his new clothes he looks distinctly ill at ease.

"If these are not sufficient, please let us know," says Doña Epiphania. "Many thanks, Doña Epiphania," says Francisco Manoel. "I have never had this many undergarments in my life." The girls giggle uncontrollably behind their fans. Doña Epiphania leaves the room, casting a disapproving look at her daughters.

In the meantime the black girl has begun washing the colonel's hair. With obvious relish, he leans his head back into a porcelain bowl that she is holding on her lap. "The thought that there are domains," he says, "that are not yet planted with my sugarcane and not yet populated by my cattle herds infuriates me. And the thought of mulatto girls I've not impregnated yet I find unbearable." He laughs and pinches his servant's hip suggestively. "Watch out for women, Francisco Manoel," the colonel says. "When do I start?" Francisco Manoel asks. "I'll show you everything," the colonel promises.

Sugarcane Fields

As far as the eye can see, the plantation stretches over gently rolling hills. The hills and valleys have a silvery glitter from the sugarcanes' beards. Octavio Coutinho and Francisco Manoel watch from a small rise as the blacks, back to back in a row without beginning or end, hack away at the yellow stalks. Their machetes glint in the sun. Their backs gleam with sweat. The sugarcane, three times taller than the men, shudders from the strike of the blade slicing through it, then, after a moment of standing motionless, of rebellion against the inevitable, bends and falls. At the points where they have been cut, the canes have jagged edges from which angry juice pours, and the leaves are so sharp that even binding their hands in rags hardly enables the slaves to protect themselves. Lacerations on their backs, blood and sweat mixing with the juice, attract swarms of black flies. The slaves bend under the weight of the sheaves of cane and stagger away, the veins in their necks swollen from the strain.

"I produce almost as much as the entire state of Pernambuco," the colonel comments. "Twenty-four thousand tons per year, and all of it goes to England, our nemesis. They've outlawed slavery there, and now they're blockading slave ships, but without us they'd have no sugar, and they take it from us as if it could be scooped out of the rivers. Grotesque."

Engenho

The sugar mill's powerful odor of molasses has attracted even larger swarms of flies. Cauldrons bubble. Yoked teams of oxen, blindfolded with sacks, turn the creaking rollers of the cane press. The pale, foaming juice is captured in large vats, and uninterruptedly new bundles of cane are thrown into the press. About a hundred slaves work here. Those tending the vats in which the boiling-off takes place are all women. The colonel leads Francisco Manoel through the bustling throng of workers.

Suddenly many silent faces turn toward a roller in which a man's hand has gotten caught. Screams; the roller cannot be reversed. An overseer who has been tugging at the man finally hacks off his hand, and the mutilated man is carried away. "Not another!" the colonel remarks and shrugs his shoulders.

The sugar mill from the outside. A tiled roof, puffing chimneys, a busy scene. In the distance the manor house, the Casa Grande, and somewhat below it the long rows of slave shacks, the *senzalas*. High above everything on a hilltop, a pretty Baroque chapel.

Going to Church

All the way up the hill the slaves stand, straw hats in hand and barefoot, forming a long row. From the manor a curious procession snakes its way toward the chapel: at its head black musicians, dancing samba steps to the rhythm of their drums; behind them, also dancing, about twenty lovely young mulatto girls, dressed up in the daintiest white lace dresses—the master's concubines. After them comes a slave carrying the cage with the parrot, screeching nonsensical sentences. Then comes the sedan chair with Octavio Coutinho. Behind him walks Doña Epiphania, accompanied by a slave with a parasol, and after her we see the three daughters in their best outfits. They are taking their marmoset to church with them and fan themselves excitedly and signal with their eyes and hands to Francisco Manoel, who follows them, walking stiff-legged in the suit of clothes he has donned under protest. Behind him come the black gardeners, the housemaids, the kitchen staff, the stable boys—children from the colonel's loins. At the end of the column the slaves who were lining the path fall in, likewise dancing.

The Manor, Veranda

A relaxed evening mood. A dense, voluptuous display of tropical flowers and plants spills from the manor's veranda into the tended, parklike gardens below. Without a sound a slave sprinkles the ground and the plants with water. Panting, Don Octavio heaves himself from his tasseled hammock and waddles off to his quarters with a young mulatto woman. "I haven't fathered any offspring today," he says. "Grotesque."

Francisco Manoel and the colonel's three daughters remain alone on the veranda. The girls are drinking fruit juices from cut crystal glasses and leafing through European fashion magazines. Francisco Manoel is noticeably silent, brooding as he repeatedly stirs a little cup of mocha. Sidelong looks, whispers, giggles, delicate suggestiveness.

Suddenly Wandeleide, the youngest, looks up because she feels

Francisco Manoel staring at her unabashedly. His gaze is so intense that the girl begins to fan herself in agitation. "So, Francisco Manoel," Valkyria says brashly, "how do the shoes fit?" Francisco Manoel remains silent. "Are you getting used to eating with knife and fork?" Bonita chimes in. "The gentleman from the Sertão," Wandeleide says, "doesn't speak. How many cows did you have?" Francisco Manoel shuts her up with a look. He continues poking at his mocha. Then all at once he gets up stiffly and makes his way down the broad steps into the garden. There he disappears in the shadow of some mango trees. At the bottom of the steps two slaves lie locked into a heavy block of wood, bearing their torment patiently. In silence they follow Francisco Manoel with their eyes.

The Garden

Wandeleide makes her way cautiously along a neatly raked garden path. She seems to be looking for something but does not want anyone to notice. A mild dusk has settled over the orchids and the shrubs' floral clusters. The day's last hummingbirds buzz around the luxuriant blossoms, then suddenly suspend their motion in midair. Wandeleide plucks a leaf from a shrub. Then, suddenly, as if risen from the ground, Francisco Manuel towers over her like a giant. She freezes, terrified by his face. His eyes are glowing. "I am Cobra Verde, the Cangaceiro," he hisses at her. "I have no need to speak." He grabs her, pulls her toward him, and kisses her wildly. She does not resist. He throws her down on a patch of lawn and tears off her blouse. She lets the beast of prey have his way, throwing her white arms around his neck.

Hummingbirds dart out of a bush and excitedly trace paths against the violet evening sky. A fiddle makes itself heard over the buzzing of their wings, followed by the hoarse voice of the balladeer:

> *The gardens confess, for secrecy has a way*
> *Of tempting young women to do themselves in.*
> *And hidden in darkness a beast of prey*
> *Crouches in shadows, on the lookout for sin.*

The year renews yearly, eleven times it has been,
His pay Cobra Verde steals from virgin after virgin.

The Manor, Entry Hall

Black chambermaids come flying in alarm out of the half-open door to the salon and huddle in a dark corner. From inside an uproar can be heard.

The Manor, Salon

The first thing we see is an overturned marble pillar whose capital held a luxuriant potted fern. The pot is broken, the fern on the parquet floor. The colonel's three daughters are weeping. Doña Epiphania is lying unconscious on an Empire chaise longue; an older maidservant sprinkles her with water. Don Octavio is beside himself. Meanwhile Francisco Manoel leans in the doorway with a cold, inscrutable expression.

"Wandeleide pregnant," screams the master of the house, "Bonita pregnant, and you, Valkyria . . . ," he pauses for a moment at the unbearable thought, then speaks very softly. "Are you also pregnant, by any chance?" "No," Valkyria sobs, "or yes, or I mean I don't know." Doña Epiphania, who has raised herself for a moment, takes the easy way out by fainting again. "A barefoot cowherd from the Sertão!" the colonel thunders, "with all of my daughters!" He marches over to Francisco Manoel. "Cowherd, what do you have to say for yourself?"

Francisco Manoel straightens up, then brings his face so close to the colonel's that they almost touch. The men lock gazes, silently murderous. "Sugarcane planter," Francisco Manoel says almost inaudibly. "I am the bandit Cobra Verde."

Veranda, Night

Nocturnal sounds from the garden. The veranda lies in darkness. Through the jalousies in the salon's windows strips of light shine onto the tiled floor, making a pattern. A murmur of voices from inside. Francisco Manoel is crouching by the window to hear the conversation inside.

Salon

Don Octavio Coutinho has gathered a group of eight fellow plantation owners for a council of war. A dense cloud of cigar smoke, cognac in cut crystal glasses. Five men are seated around a Moorish smoking table inlaid with mother-of-pearl, while the others stand. The colonel paces restlessly back and forth. "An outlaw," he says, "in my own house. A bandit, a criminal." "We'll take him to court," says the fattest man in the group. The suggestion hangs in the air for a moment but is then rejected without further discussion. "We'll kill him," says another man. "He's dangerous," says the colonel; "if we do that, we'll lose at least three or four men before we finally get him." A plantation owner at the table sips his cognac and holds the glass up to the light to examine the color. "Why don't you marry him to your daughter?" he asks. "After all, he's the best man you have on your plantation."

Francesco Manoel's eyes stare boldly through the jalousies into the room. "I'd do that," the colonel says, "but the filthy pig has impregnated all of them." "Send him to Africa to buy slaves," the fat man suggests. It takes a while for the idea to sink into the men's minds. "What do you mean, buy slaves?" the colonel asks. "It's been ten years since we've received any."

"That's just it," the fat man says. "We'd be sending him to a certain death. The king of Dahomey is insane, and everyone who's set foot on his shores has been killed. That's been the case for ten years now. No one has returned alive."

For a while the group remains silent. Yes, that's the idea. "But what if he comes back after all?" asks the colonel, not yet convinced. "He'll never manage that," says one of the men standing around the table. "And if he should manage after all," says the fat man, "he'll bring you so many slaves that you'll be able to extend your fields all the way to Sergipe. Give him your eldest daughter, get as much use out of him as possible, and as for the other two, oh, well, you'll find them husbands, I'm sure. Or you can send them to the Carmelites if you prefer." "I'm going to kill the filthy pig," says Don Octavio obstinately.

The eavesdropper's eyes glide out of the strips of light at the window and recede into the darkness.

Bahia, Great Hall of the Capitania

A bright hall whose large windows look out over the open sea. We see part of the hilly city with its three hundred churches. Here and there palm trees, splendid houses from the colonial period, clouds in the sky like balls of cotton. Nautical charts on the walls, model ships, an anchor, a heraldic crest. On the long table made of choice wood stands a large globe. About twenty men have gathered, led by the elegant governor, still very young, whose uniform with gold embroidery and gold epaulets catches our eye. Captains, officials from the harbor authority, and the plantation owners, chief among them Don Octavio in his velvet frock coat. He has an ebony walking stick with a silver knob. Facing them stands Francisco Manoel.

"Da Silva," says the governor, "we have a very special assignment for you, something we can entrust only to a highly competent man. Here are letters patent that authorize you to conduct trade in slaves. As you probably know, this trade has faltered in recent years. The king of Dahomey has broken off the deliveries, but we know that he urgently needs weapons and money. We make the following proposal: we will send you to Dahomey, to our fort in Elmina. You will be given the rank of lieutenant, and we will deposit your earnings in an account with the state bank. Five months after your departure from here, another ship will follow with a cargo of guns, with which you will pay the king. We also considered Angola, but the English have blocked the trade there, and it would be too risky. Going around the Cape to Zanzibar would also not make sense; the Arabs control the trade there."

Francisco Manoel does not reply. The others exchange conspiratorial glances. "This undertaking is very promising at present," the governor adds, "because the king of Dahomey is waging war against the Egbas. He needs us, as we need him."

"When did you last receive word from Elmina?" Francisco Manoel asks suddenly. The governor responds evasively: "That was some time ago; we no longer completely trust our people there." He pauses. "Do you accept the offer?" he asks at last.

"Yes," says Francisco Manoel without hesitation—to everyone's surprise. All those in the room cluster around him, shake his hand, and congratulate the man they think they are sending to a certain death.

"Excellent," says a beaming Don Octavio, "congratulations! Just make sure they don't cheat you by giving you bad slaves. They rub castor oil on the ones with skin diseases, and the ones who have diarrhea they plug up with oakum. Keep your eyes open."

Cheers, best wishes from all sides, a toast with port wine. We turn to an open window and gaze for a long time out over the ocean. An albatross sails by majestically.

We see billowing sails against the sky. A ship's prow forges through the blue-black sea. Then the fiddle is heard, and the song of the balladeer:

> *Keep alert and watch out for the Bay of Benin,*
> *If one makes it out, forty nevermore are seen.*

Then, because the interval in time and space will be so great and we will be entering into another world, the balladeer appears before us. We see the same godforsaken, bumpy road where he sits on his stool, almost toothless in his battered straw hat, his plywood fiddle clenched almost in the nape of his neck:

> *Eleven blazing fires, eleven weeks at sea*
> *A dead man goes forth, above clouds snow that none see.*

Africa

Swarms of jellyfish in the water, ropes of seaweed, phosphorescent particles in a current, boobies flying overhead: the weather above the oily sea is cross.

Far off on the horizon a thin, gray, disappointing strip of land, dotted very sparsely with palm trees. A little way from the shore, clearly inscribed in the water, a white line of breakers.

Francisco Manoel stands at the railing with the ship's captain looking through a spyglass. "Put me ashore," he says. "I'll take ten guns with me." "None from the crew will risk it," the captain says, "and I can't force them to go, that won't work. I'm sure they'll come and get you." Francisco Manoel hands the spyglass to the captain. "Over there on the left: what's that fellow doing?" The captain searches for a moment, then says, "I think that's one of their fetish priests praying we'll get caught in the surf. Everything that washes up on the beach becomes the property of the king, you know. They even stripped a half-drunk sailor of his clothes down to his shirt. Let's wait and see what happens."

The Beach

Far from the shore, outside the line of breakers, a large sailing ship lies motionless at anchor. We see a long black boat, a dugout, being rowed by eight Africans with frenetic strokes toward the white, foaming surf line. The boat rears into the air, then whizzes down on the foam of the mighty breaker toward the shore. A man is standing in the boat whose face we cannot quite make out, but we know it is Francisco Manoel.

In the Boat

Francisco Manoel stands erect among the muscular African rowers who speed the dugout along with rapid, rhythmic strokes. Behind the palms on the shore the sun rises, casting a reddish glow over the excited crowd waiting there.

Suddenly the rowers' precise rhythm falters. A shark has bit off almost the entire blade of one of the oars. The boat twists, fighting to stay afloat, but it does not capsize.

Above the tumbling occupants of the boat and its rearing keel we make out the great fort of Elmina.

The Beach

With a mighty swoop the boat is thrown up on the sand. Francisco Manoel pitches forward. Shouting is heard. Many hands seize the dugout and pull it out of the water before the retreating wave can suck it back in.

An aisle opens up, and silhouetted against the flaming sun appears a man on horseback. Before him come drummers and dancers, and muskets are fired into the air.

Francisco Manoel pushes aside two oarsmen who wanted to help the white man out of the boat. He refuses to climb on the shoulders of those bending their backs to carry him ashore. A fetish priest gesticulates wildly directly in front of his face.

Little puffs of musket smoke precede the rider, and around him is an inferno of shots and shouts and drumming. Now we make out a fragile eighty-year-old dressed in rose-colored silk, the yovogan, the king's minister. He is sitting sidesaddle on an emaciated gray mare, whom a servant leads by a bridle of braided grass. Another servant holds a large blue umbrella over him. Close behind him comes a noisy entourage. When servants lift him off the horse, everyone immediately falls silent. A stool is placed on the sand for him, along with a little card table and several carafes. A boy holding the old man's cigar box takes up a position beside him. Through the dust, which settles gradually, we also see a poorly shaved white man, bloated, his clothes showing white blotches from sweat. It is the missionary Bernabo. He is accompanied by several no less scruffy-looking white girls who squat down just as African girls do, their knees braced in their armpits. Bernabo, who appears to be inebriated, indicates the yovogan with his eyes, makes the throat-slitting gesture, and shakes his head at the same time. No, the new arrival will not be decapitated immediately. Francisco Manoel looks at him disdainfully; he has no need of such signals.

Instead of shaking hands to greet the stranger, the yovogan lets Francisco Manoel's fingers glide through his, then snaps his thumb and middle finger. Next he raises a glass of palm wine to the health of his king but does not drink, instead pouring the wine into the mouth of a lackey. After that water is poured and both men drink. That, says the minister, will cool the white stranger's heart.

"What about the bark full of silk?" the minister asks abruptly. "And what about the coach and horses? And the trumpets? And the silver hunting rifle?" "There are no presents," says Francisco Manoel. "Not even the greyhounds?" "Not even the greyhounds," replies Francisco Manoel. "There will be no presents until the king releases all Brazilian prisoners." "The king," the minister says, "has no more prisoners." "In that case," says Francisco Manoel, "until the fort is in full operation and the king takes up the slave trade again. I will pay with guns, with brand-new ones."

He pulls one of his guns out of a bundle wrapped in canvas and fires it. The yovogan seems much taken with it. "Our powder," he says, "speaks slowly, but this powder speaks at once." "Death to the white men!" a voice suddenly shouts from the crowd. With a single look the yovogan silences the outburst.

"Hallelujah, hallelujah," rejoices Barnabo, distributing holy wafers to some in the crowd who are kneeling. They may be converts, but they look as though they do not understand. At the end of the row an ape gets a wafer shoved into his mouth. "Hallelujah!" Musket shots, dust, pounding of drums, and the yovogan rides off though a palm grove.

Fort Elmina

The massive Portuguese fort sits on a small spit of land, next to a lovely bay with a sandy beach and slender palms. At the spot where one of the fort's bastions protrudes farthest over the sea, there is a line of palms that seems not to end until far out in the water. Several hundred meters inland, another fort occupies a hill. It is much smaller and was apparently built to ward off attacks coming from the landside.

Bernabo has attached himself to Francisco Manoel, who finds him a nuisance as he inspects the outside of the fort. The flagpole is broken, the crest damaged, in some places the roof has blown off, and the outer walls are black with smoke. The shutters dangle from their hinges, the big guns have slipped out of their mounts and partially sunk into the ground. The moat has been used as a sewer. On the drawbridge, which does not look very trustworthy, Bernabo comes out with something he has been skirting around for a while. "You'll be all right living here; the main living quarters are not too bad. And then, then you can pick out one of my daughters and take her with you into the fort."

"Are you running a brothel?" Francisco Manoel asks.

"No," says Bernabo, "I mean, it'll cost you something; I have to pay for everything here after all. But I give her only to whites. You're the first one in a long time, you know." Francisco Manoel says nothing. He enters the fort.

The Fort, Inner Courtyard

Urubus take to the air as Francisco Manoel reaches the courtyard. A pig is sniffing at a rotten fruit. A dog howls. The two long sides of the courtyard are taken up with dungeons for the slaves. A grand staircase leads up to the main living quarters, which have large windows and a roofed-over balcony. The smudges of smoke on the once whitewashed walls have been faded into streaks by rain. Clumps of grass have rooted on ledges. A patch of wild barley is growing out of the flagstones in one part of the courtyard. Cramped quarters for the soldiers, battlement walkways, empty cannon placements, vultures perched on a roof.

From the door to the chapel staggers a pockmarked fellow wearing a drum major's shako; he is an African. "Praise be to the Mother of Christ and all the saints," he says in a remarkable singsong, in which the rhythm of his native language can be detected. He touches Francisco Manoel as if to determine whether he is real.

"I am Taparica, the drum major, the only survivor from the garrison," he says. "I was a free Yoruba and joined the First Regiment of the Black Militia."

"What happened?" Francisco Manoel asks.

"It all began very strangely," Taparica tells him. "The king in Abomey is said to be not right in his head; he didn't approve of slavery. One day instead of slaves he sent a horse with only one ear. Then the king's troops attacked us. The governor was killed immediately in a skirmish on the coast, and they stormed the fort and plundered everything. The Black Militia fled, and they killed most of the whites. Now the skulls of the prisoners adorn the palace walls in Abomey. They stole everything, even the bells, and stabbed holes in the eyes of the portraits in the main living quarters. Then they pulled the plugs out of the rum casks and drank all the rum. They raped a captured cadet in the courtyard. They put ants on my chest, sprinkled pepper under my eyelids, and burned my tongue because they were convinced we had treasure buried somewhere. They were just about to kill me when one of them went into the munitions magazine with a burning torch. They pulled seven corpses out of the ruins and forgot about me."

The Spit of Land

Under the rustling palms are about thirty grave mounds, eroded by the weather. The wooden crosses, which bear no names, are weathered, some of them tipped over. Francisco Manoel climbs over the mounds, followed by Taparica.

"We don't know who is buried in which," he says, "but I think this one is the governor. Why did you come, alone and without any soldiers?" Francisco Manoel does not answer. "Aren't you afraid?" Taparica asks. "Aren't you afraid of dying?" "I never tried it," says Francisco Manoel.

Fort Elmina, Main Living Quarters

The governor's quarters. A high-ceilinged room, almost a hall, completely empty. Streaks from roof leaks down one of the walls. Taparica pushes open the wooden shutters that were temporarily nailed shut, and light floods in. Outside the crowns of palms and the sea. White foam washes up on the beach. With a long branch Taparica shoos away the bats hanging in dense clusters from the wood ceiling. They flutter around the room in confusion, then flee toward the glaring sun.

Taparica fastens a hammock to two hooks located diagonally across from each other in a corner. Francisco Manoel climbs into it, lights a cigar, and watches the smoke curl. "What do we do now?" asks Taparica. "We wait," Francisco Manoel replies.

Fort Elmina, Night

Millions of stars sparkle above the dark fort. White foam marks the surf line. Among the dark, rustling palms equally many millions of glowing dots, from glow worms. Huts, flickering embers of fires. In the ocean millions of luminescent jellyfish glow. The moon rises, large, as white as snow, and stupid. The ocean roars evenly, accompanying the vast symphony of frogs and mosquitoes. Above it all, from the sparkling universe, a strained stillness streams toward the song of the earth.

Fort Elmina, Main Living Quarters

Francisco Manoel is awakened by a din of voices and beatings. The windows are already bright with glaring, shameless daylight. Leaning over the northern bastion, Francisco Manoel sees a group of almost one hundred half-naked men who are piling up bundles of sedge, boards, baskets of oyster shells, and buckets of dried earth. At some distance sits the yovogan with his entourage. His men are beating the prisoners with sticks to keep them from slacking off in their forced labor.

Fort Elmina, Exterior

Quite a few days must have passed. Scaffoldings made of palm trunks lashed together with ropes have scaled the entire façade like vines and fastened themselves to the walls. Everywhere crews are at work, repairing, whitewashing. Dripping with sweat, blacks are passing from hand to hand baskets of filth from the moat. In the heat of the afternoon sun, which has drawn all the color out of the ground and the trees and is making the sand shimmer, Francisco Manoel da Silva is working, stripped to the waist, among the prisoners. He barks orders and shoulders even the heaviest loads.

In the courtyard the cistern gets cleaned and a door is installed. The cannons gleam from wax and palm oil. A roof is being fixed.

Taparica hesitantly brings a pitcher of water to Francisco Manoel and gives him a drink. "Never," he says, "have I seen a white man work."

The Beach

The sun rises. Boats are pushed into the foaming waves by athletic, handsome men. Suddenly all movement comes to a halt, and everyone's eyes turn toward the palm grove farther inland.

From there a long procession approaches in the morning light. We immediately realize that these are slaves. A procession of three hundred men and women with loads on their heads. The slaves are weary, yoked together with chains and iron collars. The king's soldiers drive them along, assisted by some Amazon warriors, of whom the slaves seem especially afraid. The long procession turns toward the fort when it reaches the beach.

The Ocean

Far out on the ocean a large ship lies at anchor. Several of the natives' dark boats are rowing from it toward the bay by the fort.

The Fort, Main Living Quarters

A large table laden with leftover food, glasses, port wine, and kerosene lamps that light the room. Outside the windows it is night. The few pieces of furniture do not fill the room, but they create a sense of grandeur. Slave girls, directed by Taparica, clear some of the dishes.

Francisco Manoel and a ship's captain have lit after-dinner cigars, and now they turn to business. The captain, a dark, sinewy man with sharp eyes, hands a list across the table.

"Three hundred slaves won't fill the *Fraternidade,* but it's still worthwhile. They won't believe their eyes in Bahia. Twenty percent of the profit will be credited to your account."

Francisco Manoel does not want his satisfaction to be obvious; he keeps his tone businesslike. "Guns?" he asks. "One hundred forty," says the captain, "and ammunition to go with them." "Rum?" asks Francisco Manoel. "Ten casks," says the captain. "Tobacco?" "Unfortunately it got damp and we had to throw most of it overboard." "Silk?" "Five rolls, not the best quality, but no one here will notice." "I'll need more guns next time. The northern border seems to have a lot of unrest, and apparently the Egbas won a battle. But the reports we get are very incomplete; I'm guessing from various indications."

"May I allow myself a personal observation?" the captain asks after a pause during which he toys with his wine glass. Francisco Manoel encourages him with an economical gesture. "If I may say so, we were prepared for all sorts of possibilities, but that you would manage here . . . how do you explain it that they're willing to send you slaves?"

"I don't know," says Francisco Manoel. "I think they need me."

A Lagoon

A seemingly endless procession of slaves is wading through a wide lagoon. They are dead tired, the iron collars have rubbed their skin raw. Loads on their heads. The beginning of the human chain cannot be made out among the native huts and the palms on the beach, which can be glimpsed at a distance between their trunks, nor can the end somewhere in the landscape. Detachments of guards on donkeys, whose backs barely rise above the water of the ford, beat the prisoners to keep them moving. This via dolorosa seems to cover an entire continent.

Beneath the palms stands Francisco Manoel with Taparica, watching the slaves pass. "The best way to tell their age," Taparica says, "is by looking at their gums." "There are more and more of them," Francisco Manoel says. "The more guns we send, the bigger the war becomes, and then there are more and more prisoners, and the king needs even more guns." "They're the lucky ones," Taparica says; "we save people who otherwise would be sacrificed in the annual ritual; they would be dispatched to the other world as messengers to the ancestors. Now they're sent to a wonderful country where all the people dance and cigars grow on trees."

Francisco Manoel is the first to notice that something is amiss, that something unusual is taking place. Men from the village break into a run, children flee in horror, only a few women have stayed behind. They have seized a goat and are holding it to the ground, bending its head back. They sacrifice the goat, cutting its throat. "It's night, night!" shout the women as the goat's life gurgles out of its body.

And now we too see that porters are carrying something across the lagoon, a hammock into which a person has been sewn. Four men carry the pole from which the hammock is suspended, holding it above their heads.

"Find out what's going on," Francisco Manoel instructs Taparica.

Taparica disappears among the huts. We see the hammock reach the shore and be placed in a large boat. The person inside is moving.

Taparica comes back to Francisco Manoel. "It's Bossa Gelele," he says, "the king's older brother. All men and children in the country who have the name Bossa are to be killed."

"Why?" Francisco Manoel asks.

"The king," Taparica says, "can't stand to have anyone else in his kingdom bear his given name. He is called Bossa, Bossa Ahadee. He can't kill his own brother in his country, so he's going to be drowned at sea."

Fort, Inner Courtyard

The courtyard is packed with the new slaves, who are being placed in the separate dungeons for men and women. A man who appears half-dead is released from his chains and laid in a corner. A strangely tense atmosphere has settled over Francisco Manoel and his few people. Something is in the air.

The rumble of drums. Shouts that sound threatening. The

yovogan hurries in through the main gate with his entire retinue, preceded by an Amazon warrior. As if beside herself she waves a banner in Francisco Manoel's face. A large sunshade is twirled above the minister's head. Without beating around the bush, he tells Francisco Manoel, "If the king is looking for someone, no one is allowed to hide. If someone takes refuge underground, the ground speaks."

Francisco Manoel remains outwardly calm in the face of this declaration. At the gate all those in the vicinity suddenly throw themselves on their knees and humbly toss dust on their heads. A messenger from the king, his head shorn on one side and insignia on his clothing, approaches rapidly on foot. He is carrying a royal staff in his hands, with his arms straight out in front of him; as it passes, everyone in the inner courtyard prostrates himself—the slaves, the Black Guard, the yovogan with his retinue; only Francisco Manoel remains standing. The messenger lays the staff on the ground, lies down flat, and repeats the message he has learned by heart. At the end of every sentence, he makes a mark in the sand with his finger. "The leopard," he says, "has fathered a son with a human female. The son's temples still show traces of his paws. The leopard's son says he loves the new white man too much. Is the white man in good health? The king will smash his foes. On the stomach of the king of the Egbas he will erect his new palace. The white man comes from over the sea. He has seen many things. The king has laid out a royal road for him. The king wishes to see the stranger."

The messenger, still on the ground, hands a letter to Francisco Manoel, who bends to receive it, opens it, and reads. "The king," the messenger says, "had his scribe write this for you." As Francesco Manoel studies the letter, his face becomes remarkably tranquil. We see the sheet of paper. We read, "I, Antonio Maciel, Portuguese, have for sixteen years been a prisoner of this cruel king without ever seeing one of my fellow countrymen. Beware and do not come; it will be your death."

"This is your pass," the messenger says and hands Francisco Manoel a pouch into which he places a smooth round stone. By way of confirmation, he cuts a wedge in another, somewhat simpler, staff. Francisco Manoel thus gains some time for reflection. "Tell His Majesty," he says, "that one of my feet must be in the ocean. I cannot come."

Francisco Manoel cannot even finish because at that an incredible hubbub breaks out. The yovogan's entourage jumps Francisco Manoel and knocks him to the ground. The Black Guard flees in a panic. With a foot on his throat, Francisco Manoel fights for breath and opens his mouth. A wooden gag is forced down his throat and his hands and feet are bound. One of his boots is yanked off, and his foot is stuck in a earthenware pitcher of seawater. He is sewn into a hammock, with only his head sticking out. He chokes on the gag. Next to him Taparica is tied up and sewn completely into a hammock.

Road

The road is more like an interweaving of several dusty footpaths. Trees here and there, and between them fields where women are working, their backs bent, with short-handled hoes. Along the way a group of people with bundles of dry wood on their heads. A troop of at least twenty men comes running toward them. The men are armed, and running on ahead of them is the king's messenger with the royal staff. The women scatter to the side, far into the fields.

Village

A native village at the foot of an overhanging cliff with a small waterfall. Odd mud huts with very little floor space, pointed straw roofs, granaries, everything crowded together right up to the base of the cliffs. On the edge of the village wooden racks nailed together to form a succession of gates, from which corpses have been hung by their feet. To the left and right posts topped with skulls.

The troop with the two hammocks rushes by, changing bearers without stopping. The village's inhabitants flee as the troop passes through the gates.

River

A wide, brown, sluggish river, the landscape on either side withered from drought. Sparse vegetation consisting of spindly shrubs, on which a herd of goats is grazing. In the air yellowish dust from a distant desert. Two goatherds wearing long robes and wide, funnel-shaped hats take cover behind withered bushes.

Abomey

Against the evening sky, a causeway with pools of flat, muddy water on either side. On the dam the high-water line from the rainy season. In the distance we see Abomey, the royal residence. Flat, cube-shaped mud houses, and towering above them the imposing palace, also made of mud. In between a few palm trees. A city like the kind of oasis one sees in dreams of a distant unknown planet.

The troop with the prisoners trots along the causeway.

Abomey, Streets

The city is mysterious and exotic. Irregular streets thread their way among the almost windowless mud houses. We accompany the troop. People peer down from flat roofs, pulling their heads back as the procession approaches. Children disappear into doorways and women take to their heels.

Abomey, Dungeon

An inner courtyard surrounded by high mud walls topped with skulls. A building with a dark entryway in which only the whites of eyes can be seen staring. A tree with spindly branches casts a spotty shadow on the dusty ground but provides no relief from the heat. Hellish twittering of weaverbirds.

Francisco Manoel has been tied in a sitting position to a post. A wooden rod has been inserted under his knees. The crooks of his arms are under the rod, and his hands are tied over his shins, making him into a completely immobilized package. The gag has been removed from his mouth. Flies buzz around his face, whose skin is cracked from the dryness. Next to him is Taparica, bound in the same manner. His teeth are chattering, to the extent that teeth as irregular as his can chatter. Along a wall, where a sharp, narrow strip of shade can be found, squat several armed men, the guard unit.

As we move in closer, we see that Francisco Manoel's foot is still stuck in the earthenware pitcher. On the dusty ground crouches a fat frog that lurches toward the moist container. Then the frog sits still, spent, as if its heart were about to burst from the effort of that one hop.

Francisco Manoel's inflamed, encrusted eyes squint as he tries to take in his surroundings. Slowly he turns his head toward Taparica, still able to muster some encouragement. "I wish I had your skin," he says. The blacks believe the devil is white.

Abomey, Square in Front of the Palace

The large central square in Abomey, bordered by the cube-shaped mud houses, with the mighty royal palace looming over it. Three massive towers, Moorish ramparts, everything built of light-colored mud. A low mud wall encircles the building, which is topped with skulls. Shallow steps paved with skulls lead up to the main portal. On the sandy square a large crowd has gathered.

Seated on a stool facing the steps is Francisco Manoel, still bound and with his foot in the pitcher. Next to him, also tied up, sits Taparica.

On one side, coming from the palace, a large procession appears: drummers, dancers, soldiers, among them Amazons, brandishing their curved bush knives, eunuchs, high officials with bodyguards. The officials stand out because broad sunshades are being twirled over their heads. Heralds, ambassadors from other African peoples in splendid robes, several hundred women, the king's seraglio. They all squat on the square. Many of the men are smoking black tobacco in short-stemmed pipes. Lackeys sweep the sandy ground clean for the king. Dancing soldiers toss their muskets into the air in unison, catch them, and then, holding them in both hands, leap over them. Shots, drum rolls, the racket and chaos becoming increasingly infernal.

Then, from one moment to the next, silence, and into the silence a shout: "Attention! The leopard is coming!" The thousands of people in the square fall on their faces, toss dust on themselves, kiss the ground. Francisco Manoel is knocked over, together with his stool, his face in the sand.

The king makes his entrance, followed by lackeys, his favorite wives, the royal household guard, heralds, a spittoon bearer, and a slave turning a gigantic umbrella over him. The umbrella is adorned with human jawbones. Kankpé, his insane brother, is with him, likewise with an entourage.

Bossa Ahadee, the king, raises his staff. His subjects' shrieking becomes ecstatic. "Dada! Breathe for me! Rob me! Dada! Dada! Break me! Take me! My head is yours!"

The king, a large, sinewy man with dry, reddened eyes, has the mechanical gestures and jovial air of a practiced slaughterer. His long fingernails curve, his feet are clad in sandals woven of gold wire, his clothing is simple but splendid. Servants fan him constantly. He takes a seat on a stool. Two freshly harvested heads are deposited before him. "The leopard has risen," a herald proclaims. "Two messengers have been sent forth to report it to the ancestors in the Other World." To one side of and a bit behind him, Kankpé also takes a seat. Then something remarkable happens. Directly next to the king a second throne stool is placed, and in front of it empty gold sandals. No one sits there, but this no one has an entourage just like the king's. Servants fan him, a sunshade is swung over his head, a spittoon is placed beside him. "The bush king," proclaims the herald, "is taking his seat." More tossing of sand by the crowd, the same cries, the same displays of humility. Now heralds shout the king's Strong Names.

Francisco Manoel and Taparica next to him are roughly set upright. The water in the pitcher has drained away into the sand. Sand clings to Francisco Manoel's face.

A mighty wooden drum is pounded. The crowd falls silent.

A herald near the king begins to shout. "The leopard speaks! Before the annual ritual, before the gate of tears all dogs must be killed in the night. The dogs gather in the streets and try to speak like humans. If they succeed, they will bring pestilence over the people!"

A servant reverently picks up the empty sandals, comes to Francisco Manoel, and places them on the ground before him. The sun shade circles above the sandals. A glass of palm wine is poured, then dumped into the sand. "What is this, what does it mean?" Francisco Manoel whispers to Taparica. "That's the bush king," Taparica whispers in reply. "He exists only in the imagination, but he rules, too."

Now the real king rises from his seat. "We must defeat the Egbas," he exclaims. "We will break Abeokeouta! My house needs roofing!" Frenetic cheers greet these utterances, shouts of "We will cover your roof with the skulls of the enemy!"

Bossa Ahadee approaches Francisco Manoel, and his entire retinue moves with him. He stops directly in front of Francisco Manoel. Another glass of palm wine is poured, then emptied into Francesco Manoel's mouth. For the king a bowl made out of a skull is filled. As he prepares to drink, he is shrouded in cloths. The entire crowd on the square turns away. "When the lion drinks," proclaims the herald, "he does not permit the other animals to watch!" The cloths are removed. The king's drunkard kneels, and the remaining wine is poured into his open mouth. "How fare my relatives?" asks Bossa Ahadee. "Answer, white man, before I kill you. How fares the king of Prussia, how fares my brother, the czar of Russia? And how fares the great calabash overflowing with palm wine for the thirsty man, Queen Victoria?" "I can't hear you," replies Francisco Manoel, "because you are such thunder." This remark elicits from the king a brittle, tobacco-stained smile. He thinks for a moment, then smashes the earthenware pitcher with his staff and cuts the prisoner's fetters. Francisco Manoel stands before him, his face battered, his wrists swollen, the bootless foot swollen and wrinkled from the salt water. "Wait for death, stranger," says the king, "no time catches the king unawares."

Prison Yard

With the gusto and intense concentration of children, several soldiers are busy dipping Francisco Manoel into a barrel of indigo
dye. To be certain that the color penetrates every pore, they hold
his head under for a while, letting him breathe through a straw.
"The devil is white, death is white!" they chortle. "All whites are
as good as half-dead!"

They yank him out of the dye and throw him onto the sand
next to Taparica, then pour water from a leather pail over him to
check whether the dark dye holds. One of them scrubs his face, but
his skin emerges gray, only somewhat darker, from the scrubbing.

"They always do that," Taparica explains, "when they behead
a white person. They dye you because they're not allowed to kill
any white person."

Francisco Manoel fights for breath. Large black millipedes
crawl over him. "Here the dead are more alive than the living,"
he says.

Palace, Throne Room

The large, almost empty throne room of mud; the floor is fine
sand. The only noticeable ornamentation consists of wonderful
decorations in white around the doors. The entire middle of the
floor is paved with human skulls. Around the base of the walls
is a bright line fashioned of skull bones. On a shallow platform,
likewise made of skulls, sits Bossa Ahadee on a throne that is
actually just a handsomely adorned stool. The empty throne with
the sandals is next to him, and to his left sits Kankpé. Above
all three mighty personages the umbrellas are twirled, although
no sun penetrates here. Half-naked women from the seraglio,
eunuchs, lackeys, and a few strange figures in white, flowing
robes. They beat their arms like wings and now and then utter
twittering sounds. These are the king's birds.

Francisco Manoel has been positioned, unfettered, before
the king at some distance. He is missing a boot, and his skin is
blueish-gray. He seems calm, almost cold.

The king deigns to play with his prisoner. He comes to him and holds out a polished human brain pan, its edges rimmed with brass. "Ha, white man," he says by way of greeting, "I will drink from your skull, too, someday. This here was the king of the Mahis."

The king has food and drink placed at Francisco Manoel's feet, but he does not touch them. To prove that they are not poisoned, the king has his taster sample them. When Francisco Manoel still refuses to move, the king has the dishes handed to him. He shakes the cornmeal mush over his left shoulder. "That is how the dead eat," he says. Then he pours out the palm wine over his right shoulder. "That is how the dead drink."

Francisco Manoel stands stiffly, his eyes seeming to search for something in the distance. Then he notices the gaze of Kankpé, who, numbly in the grip of his insanity, is rolling his eyes, apparently sending some signal.

"I have sworn in my house of oaths," the king says, "to exterminate the Egbas. I fear no one. I have but one fear—that someday I will have nothing left in the world to conquer. But tell me, white man, why has Portugal sent three hundred thirty-five thousand warships to my coast? And why did you poison my greyhound?"

That is enough to make the guards hurl themselves at Francisco Manoel. He is beaten, kicked, and knocked to the ground. He utters not a sound. Guinea hens that were roaming the room scatter in all directions.

Prison Yard

It is nighttime, and the yard is brightly lit by the moon. Half-dead and battered, Francisco Manoel lies on the ground staring into the sky. "Snow, snow," he whispers.

The guards have fallen asleep in a seated position. One of them is startled awake by a sound, but it is already too late. Dark figures swing themselves over the wall, jump into the yard, and fall upon the surprised guards. A short skirmish, tumult, shouts, death rattles, then it is all over.

Francisco Manoel is pulled to his feet. "Quick, come along, stranger," a man says to him in the darkness. "I am Bakoko, Prince Kankpé's confidant. He is waiting for you." "Where is Taparica?" asks Francisco Manoel.

Abomey, House Roofs

The escape takes place in silence across the flat mud roofs. People sleeping there on mats wake up with a start. Francisco Manoel is lifted over a wall. Among the hurrying figures we make out Taparica, the drum major.

Abomey, Alleys

Around a corner in the twisted alleys the group of escapees comes running; there are twenty in all. A man who happens to get in their way is mowed down. Behind them at a distance we hear a hue and cry and a musket being fired.

The Bush

By the first light of dawn we recognize the jagged cliffs that extend all the way across the plain to the horizon. Boulders strewn about, sparse bushes, a mighty baobab tree, whose gray bark suggests an elephant's skin. A fire is glowing. This place seems to be safe. We recognize Kankpé first by his large sun shade, next to him Bakoko, and across from them Francisco Manoel and Taparica. Above them large birds perched on the tree's dead branches. Kankpé seems to be somewhere else; his confidant speaks for him, possibly just using the insane man for his own purposes.

"Prince Kankpé," he says, "has decided to revolt against his brother; he is the rightful heir to the throne. In Abimilakrou a woman bore a son who was half-leopard, that was our sign. Yesterday Bossa Ahadee set off with his entire army to the north."

"There," Kankpé unexpectedly interrupts him, "live many hills." Francisco Manoel, his face still darkened by the dye, looks at him in astonishment.

"We will defeat Bossa, and for that we need you. You will teach us how to use the new guns," Bakoko says.

"The soldiers will run away in alarm when they hear the sound of their own shots," Francisco Manoel says doubtfully. A pause ensues. Bakoko, a slim man with intelligent eyes, is thinking. In the distance a leopard hisses. "My father," Kankpé says.

"The traitor Bossa must be killed," Bakoko resumes. "He has opened the graves of the ancestors. He spat a mouthful of rum into the face of the mingan, the prime minister. He castrated a soldier because his hips were too wide. He had the belly of one of his wives cut open to prove that her child was male. We will go with you to the fortress on the coast, and there we will assemble an army. Here and now Kankpé wants to make you his blood brother. Blood brothers cannot kill each other; they die together."

Francisco Manoel reaches a decision. "If the new king will give me the slave trade, I'm ready." Bakoko searches the face of Prince Kankpé, who is staring straight ahead. "He agrees," he says, "he says yes."

Banyan Tree

Kankpé and Francisco Manoel kneel under the spreading shade of a banyan tree, both of them naked, their bodies pressed together. They are alone. Kankpé reaches into his leather pouch and pulls out a bowl made from a skull. He places it between their knees and pours in the sacramental ingredients: ashes, beans, baobab marrow, a thunderstone, a bullet removed from a corpse, and the powdered head of a horn viper. He fills the bowl half-full with water. Then each man slits one of the other's fingers. They press the fingers together and watch the dark blood drip into the bowl.

Fort Elmina, Beach

The light comes up. We see the beach, the ocean, Fort Elmina in the distance. The preparations for war are in full swing. About two thousand men are practicing hand-to-hand combat. Francesco

Manoel stands beside the banner, the symbol of revolt, made from a remnant of scarlet silk, torn into long strips. Taparica comes along with a troop of young, fierce-looking women, all armed with terrifying curved bush knives. "That's good," says Francisco Manoel, "from now on, only women. The men are useless for fighting."

And now, upon closer inspection, we realize that without exception all the warriors on the beach are women, an entire army of Amazons, making as if to attack each other with gruesome ferocity. Before us a huge battle rages. Francisco Manoel bellows at them, and the women warriors immediately call a halt. "In formation!" Francisco Manoel shouts. But the women do not succeed in organizing themselves into military ranks. All that results is hopeless pushing and shoving, producing a disorganized heap rather than a formation. "I have to learn how to handle them," Francisco Manoel sighs. "I must teach them to do what they do best. We're all going to rest now," he shouts, "until the sun is this high." He places his outstretched arm in his other hand in such a way as to create a perfect angle. He sees that he is understood. The warriors set out for the fort.

Palm Grove, Spit of Land by the Fort

Bakoko, Francisco Manoel, and several dignitaries are seated on mats in the shadow of the palms near the old grave mounds. In the background Amazons can be seen in all imaginable positions of midday idleness. Now and then one of them glances over at the men. Bakoko is gazing calmly straight ahead, chewing on nuts. From Francisco Manoel's alarmed gaze we now realize that they are all fixated on the same thing, and only Francisco Manoel's reaction is noticeable amid the general equanimity. "If," Bakoko says, still chewing, "all of our king's wives take each other by the hand, they will reach from border to border of the country."

Now we see what Francisco Manoel has been staring at so strangely. Not far from him, Kankpé is just getting up from embracing a young woman, who sits up part of the way and grabs a chicken from a nearby hollow in the sand she dug to keep cool.

She pulls out a feather and calmly pokes around in her ear with it. "Our king Kankpé wishes to give his blood brother a gift," says Bakoko. "He has just fathered a prince for him."

Village on the Shore

The time has come for the evening meal. Many fires are smoking among the natives' huts. The Amazon army is encamped. Some of the women are scooping barley beer from calabashes, others are frying beignets in palm oil, while others wrap cornmeal mush in banana leaves. Near us agoutis are being roasted over the fire—rats almost the size of beavers, with yellow teeth. A long procession of women arrive with bundles of firewood on their heads.

Francisco Manoel appears among his warriors. "Tomorrow," he says, "will be a long day. You will practice hard." He cannot continue because an Amazon leaps to her feet in front of him and attacks an imaginary foe with terrifying blows. "No more practicing—we want to fight!" she shouts. Several others jump up, their eyes ferocious. "We swear," they shout, "to bring you the head of Bossa Ahadee. If we have to go through burning fire, we will! If the enemy takes to the air, we will fly! If he dives underwater, we will follow him! If he sinks into the ground, we will go down after him!"

The entire encampment rises up in an indescribable tumult. Francisco Manoel is helpless to stop it and well pleased.

Open Area in Front of the Fort

In the area in front of the fort the Amazon army has divided into two approximately equal divisions that have taken up positions facing each other. Oppressive heat, the air filled with the awful yellowish dust of the Harmattan, has settled over everything. Francisco Manoel and the two female generals are standing between the army divisions. They raise glasses of Dutch gin in a toast. "No firing, not a sound, not a single word while we are on the march. We three will keep away from the roads, each of us going separately." "I will storm Abomey all by myself," says one of the Amazon generals. "I will bring the traitor's head." They empty their glasses. The two Amazons smash their glasses on the ground. "That's how we'll break if we don't attack the enemy bravely."

That was apparently the signal for the two parts of the army to hurl themselves at each other. A dreadful pseudo-slaughter breaks out. What strikes us as most strange is that it all takes place in complete silence. Then in a flash the terrible battle breaks off when Francisco Manoel fires a shot in the air.

The Causeway

Some distance off we see the city of Abomey, toward which the road atop the dam leads directly. A delegation of fetish priests carefully lays a python across the road; they throw themselves down on the ground before the snake, then withdraw a bit. Now we also see at whom this action is aimed: from the opposite direction Francisco Manoel's Amazon army approaches, at its head the two female generals, Kankpé, Bakoko, and Francisco Manoel.

"They have taken the sacred python out of the temple," Bakoko says. "We must turn back." "Why?" Francisco Manoel asks. "No one passes the python alive." "In the country I come from," says Francisco Manoel, "I was a snake myself." To the horror of all the others, he goes up to the animal and pushes it aside with his boot. The fetish priests flee; the spell is broken. With shrill cries the Amazon army storms forward.

Abomey, Roofs

Over the flat mud roofs of the city, a wild pursuit is in progress. The Amazons seem to be everywhere. The government soldiers flee in panic; only those who are trapped turn to face them and are mowed down mercilessly. On one roof a wild skirmish breaks out that continues in the alley below.

On the great square in front of the royal palace soldiers of the guard run agitatedly back and forth, firing their muskets before aiming properly at their enemies. Then they flee before the Amazons with their bush knives reach them.

Palace, Throne Room

Bossa Ahadee is sitting with stoic equanimity on his throne-stool. With him are only a few eunuchs. No one is waiting on him anymore, which immediately becomes noticeable because the umbrella above the imaginary bush king continues to be turned and the nonexistent king continues to be fanned.

Amazons storm in, followed by Francisco Manoel and Bakoko, who stop in their tracks. Then Kankpé strides through the door with unusual gravity, his eyes empty, his mind elsewhere.

"The dead kings have deposed you," the eunuchs exclaim and pull the apathetic Bossa Ahadee's sandals of gold wire off his feet. Bossa Ahadee stands up and turns to leave. "I will take a nap," he says, and leaves through the door to his seraglio. "Wall up the door to the seraglio," he says without turning his head.

"Take him prisoner," Francisco Manoel says. "No," says Bakoko, "he's going to have his wives strangle him."

The eunuchs throw themselves on the ground and toss handfuls of dust on their heads in an extravagant display of humility. Kankpé is led to the stool and seated, and his feet are put in the sandals. In his numbness he seems to become a little more lively. He whispers something to Bakoko, who throws himself on the ground in front of Francisco Manoel and kisses the sand. "He has given you the name Adjinakou," he says, "the snake." He has made you viceroy of Dahomey. Our King Kankpé gives you Fort Elmina as your residence."

More and more Amazon warriors have crowded into the room and toss dust over themselves on the ground. A stool is placed next to the new king, and Francisco Manoel, led by the eunuchs, is seated on it.

Elmina, Battlement Walk

The evening sun between the palms on the shore. Below the fort's walls blacks are busy putting in plantings while others work on piping in water. Francisco Manoel, equipped with a royal staff, seems calm and relaxed. The old yovogan, demoted to a lackey, is fanning him. Taparica has a new uniform, allowing the inference that he has been promoted.

"Those new glass windows in the main living quarters," says Francisco Manoel, "are to be removed tomorrow. The servants poured water on them because they thought the rising sun had set them on fire." "Yes, Adjinakou," says Taparica. "And then make sure the ventilation for the slaves is improved; too many are dying." "Yes, Adjinakou." "If only we could ship them off more quickly," says Francisco Manoel. "I'll build a dock, and in a year we'll have both of the ships I ordered in Bahia."

They wander along the battlement with the cannon emplacements. "Is the captain of the *Flor de Bahia* lodged comfortably?" asks Francisco Manoel. "Yes, Adjinakou," says Taparica, "he has the east wing." "Has the convoy to Abomey been readied?" "Yes," says Taparica, "tomorrow all will be in position. The distance is twenty-three thousand five hundred bamboo staffs; it will be a surprise for our king."

Elmina, the Slave Quarters

Together with the captain of the *Flor de Bahia*, Francisco Manoel is inspecting the dungeons of the male slaves. The captain is a large-boned man with ponderous gestures.

Into a long, vaulted space into which very little light filters, almost four hundred slaves have been packed. They are lying and squatting so close together that not a patch of ground can be seen. Although they are locked in, they are wearing heavy chains, and many have bloody welts on their backs. Silence as all the slaves fix their eyes on the two men. In the dim light it looks as though the space is occupied only by eyes.

"In Bahia you've been offered a seat in the syndicate," the captain says. "I don't need the seat," says Francisco Manoel, "but why do I still not have the patents for my ships?" "I don't know," says the captain, and it sounds as though he is lying, "but I'll put in a word with the governor right away." "It's also not right," Francisco Manoel says, "that the governor, as you say, doesn't authorize the deliveries of goods and weapons. You're getting the second shipment of slaves, yet I've received nothing in return. I have nothing in hand, so I'm forced to rely on your word."

Elmina, Small Courtyard

Directly behind the building with the main living quarters is a small, irregularly shaped courtyard. From there a gateway leads to the dungeon in which the female slaves are housed. Up above, three stories up, a balcony along the quadrangle's parapet has several entrances to the living quarters. Down in the courtyard about two hundred slaves are gathered. They are looking up at the balcony, where Francisco Manoel and the captain are standing.

"Sometimes," Francisco Manoel says, "I'm sick of it. Tonight I'm not going to take one of them. Which one do you want?" The captain looks down on the crowd. Finally he points to a young, very beautiful woman. Francisco Manoel waves to her, a ritual that seems to be well established. "If she gets pregnant, she won't be shipped out," he says. "In that case she'll be given a hut out there. We already have a whole village."

From the courtyard, two-stage ladders give access to the balcony, onto which one can climb through a heavy hatch made of beams, locked from above. The young slave woman climbs up while all the others are driven back to their dungeon. The captain opens the hatch, following his prize for the night with greedy eyes as she climbs toward him. "What kind of women are these?" he asks. Francisco Manoel stares into the courtyard, empty by now. "Our future murderers," he says.

Elmina, East Bastion

The east bastion, equipped with several cannons, faces inland. Somewhat to the side of it, on a hill, we can see the light-colored smaller fort. Clear morning air. From the ocean wafts a breeze.

Francisco Manoel, Taparica, and the captain are standing on the bastion and looking out over the land. Taparica has a flag in his hand. Following the direction of the three men's gaze, we catch sight of something surprising. As far as the eye can see, uphill and downhill, disappearing into the countryside and reappearing farther off, we see a long line of people, posted at intervals of one to two hundred meters, depending on the terrain. They too are holding flags. "Taparica," says Francisco Manoel, "the signal." Taparica waves a signal with the flag, and it is promptly taken up by the first flag bearer at the fort, repeated by the next one, and then the next one, like a wave; it moves along at the speed of lightning, disappears in a dip, and reappears on the brow of the hill on the other side. In twenty seconds the signal has already traveled ten or twelve kilometers, until it is lost from sight far in the distance.

"I'll write a letter for you to give to my partners," Francisco Manoel says, turning to the captain, who looks confused. "It'll take at least an hour and a half anyway for an answer to our signal to come back."

Great Hall

Francisco Manoel sits alone at a table writing. The size of the room allows us to sense the dimensions of his loneliness. We see the letter as his hand moves along:

> How should I begin to describe this humdrum life of mine? How to describe the loneliness of being without a family and friends? To be the only white man in this country, perhaps on this continent. By now I have fathered sixty-two children, but it gives me no satisfaction. Perhaps I shall return next year and marry.
>
> I would like to live in countries with ice and snow, it matters not where, so long as it is not here . . .

Taparica startles him out of his reverie. "Adjinakou, an answer is coming."

East Bastion

With a large spyglass Francisco Manoel looks out across the countryside. We see what he is seeing, compressed at a great distance a broad surface with sparse bushes, the ground flickering with heat, wavering with reflections above a sea of mirages. In the flickering, the string of people, pulsing from heat and fever, gets lost. From the deepest depths of the landscape, at first grotesquely distorted by surges of fire, a flag signal moves along, as fast as the abrupt flight of an unknown prehistoric bird, becoming increasingly clear and distinct. Francisco puts down the spyglass. Two hills away the signal disappears for brief moments, then suddenly it is close by and sweeps up to the fort. Taparica is the last to repeat it; it is different from the one sent out. "The king," he says, "sends his brother the Great Leopard Salute."

Elmina, by the Fort

Francisco Manoel is supervising the laying out of a plantation at the foot of the fort. Something seems to have gone wrong with the water level when the irrigation canal was graded. Black slaves are digging it deeper in one section, removing the earth in baskets.

A man approaches. As he gets closer, we recognize Bernabo, the missionary, who looks even more disheveled than before. "Where have you been?" Francisco Manoel asks him, surprised. "I decided I preferred to retire to somewhere quieter when it got so unsettled here," Bernabo says. "I was in Lagos, which is now firmly in the hands of the English." He assumes a mysterious expression. "You know Pedro Vicente?" he asks. "Yes," says Francisco Manoel, "the captain of the *Flor de Bahia*." "How much would an interesting piece of news be worth to you?" Bernabo asks. "That depends," says Francisco Manoel, "I'm reliable when it comes to paying." "Pedro Vicente," says Bernabo, "took slaves from you without paying, right?" Francisco Manoel nods, astonished. Bernabo seems to know the details. "Can you guess what I saw with my own eyes? Pedro Vicente had the ship fully loaded; he defrauded you. He sold off the goods and the weapons to the English."

Francisco Manoel reflects for a moment, very collectedly. "And do you know what happened with the *Flor de Bahia*?" Bernabo asks rhetorically.

"Tell me," says Francisco Manoel.

"The ship is anchored off Lagos, no longer seaworthy, and the crew has mutinied. Now you have him trapped." "Take a cutter to Lagos this very day," Francisco Manoel says, "and bring the captain of the *Flor de Bahia* a message from me: come to Elmina and I will get you afloat again. No one defrauds me twice."

Elmina, Inner Courtyard

The great gate swings open and a guard detachment enters the courtyard first, as is customary with slave transports. Francisco Manoel is waiting there with Taparica and some soldiers of his Black Guard, prepared to receive the slaves. But something very unusual happens. Instead of a procession of slaves, a small group of cripples crawls in, chained together with iron collars like slaves. Surprisingly, the cripples are accompanied by Bakoko, a much higher official than escorted previous transports. With Bakoko come several royal tax collectors, who immediately make their way uninvited into the fort's main living quarters.

Francisco Manoel needs a moment to collect himself. "What does this mean?" he asks. "Our king, Kankpé," comes the reply, "was never insane; he just feigned insanity. He thanks the one who was his brother, whom he elevated to viceroy. The king's blood brother, he has asked me to report, was a Great Tree." "Why," asks Francisco Manoel, "does the king speak of me only in the past tense?"

But he receives no answer. His Black Guard makes itself scarce. From the main building the tax agents haul away a money chest, guns, a carpet. They are looting freely. Bakoko turns and leaves. Francisco Manoel, who appears for the first time shocked and at a loss, gazes uncertainly at Taparica. "Adjinakou," he says, "it looks very bad, but you are safe from King Kankpé. He will never kill a blood brother."

Great Hall

Francisco Manoel is sitting at the table as if lost, completely preoccupied with his thoughts; before him stands Pedro Vicente, the captain of the *Flor de Bahia,* looking indecisive. "You actually want to help me?" he says at last. "I keep my word," says Francisco Manoel. Another long silence ensues. Both men's thoughts seem to be somewhere else.

"That won't help me at this point, or you either," the captain says suddenly. Francisco Manoel looks at him. All at once the hulking man bursts out, "Brazil," says Pedro Vicente, "has also abolished slavery. Any transports that are still under way will be seized at sea. Officially Fort Elmina and our way of life have ceased to exist. And another thing, now that I'm at it: I've known for a year that you're slandered and betrayed by your partners in Bahia. Your fortune has been confiscated by the state bank. In addition, the English have placed a price on your head." "So something's happened at last," says Francisco Manoel. He takes a piece of paper lying in front of him, tears it in shreds, pours himself a glass of champagne, and swallows the paper with it. "That," he says, "was my contract with the syndicate in Bahia." He pours himself another glass and one for the captain, then he gets up from the table. The two lost men look each other in the eye. They clink glasses. "To slavery," says Pedro Vicente, "to the greatest misunderstanding in the history of mankind!"

"It was no misunderstanding," Francisco Manoel replies, "it was a great crime. It will never be abolished with laws. Slavery is a characteristic of the human heart. To our downfall!"

The two men drain their glasses at one gulp. "What are you going to do?" asks the captain. "I will go to Abomey," says Francisco Manoel. "Where else can I still go?"

Elmina, Drawbridge

Early morning, the sky hidden by rain-drenched clouds blowing inland from the ocean. Not a soul far and wide, no sound, only the wind rustling in the palms.

Francisco Manoel comes out of the gate. He is carrying his royal staff and a meager bundle over his shoulder. Taparica follows him. Once arrived at the drawbridge, the two men stop briefly and take leave of each other, without words. Taparica remains behind, giving a military salute. Francisco Manoel seems confused, almost absent-minded. He hurries away, heading inland.

A Village

A village with odd, straw-roofed huts lies in the humid heat of the day, with not a person in sight. The defeated Francisco Manoel comes striding along, holding his head high.

In the center of the village, which widens into a dusty square, a group of young men comes toward him, having apparently been expecting him. They are slim, extraordinarily handsome figures wearing splendidly ornamented long robes. They have painted their faces with care, almost like women. They have jewelry woven into their hair. They are young Geerewols, who move forward with swaying dance steps, twisting their faces to reveal their gleaming teeth and rolling their eyes to show the whites. It is as if they have been ordered up, organized for the wanderer's benefit.

Francisco Manoel does not allow himself to be detained. He walks straight through the group of dancers, who step aside to let him pass. "The Great Tree falls," one of the handsome fellows calls out.

Abomey

Timidly, like a nocturnal animal harshly forced to face the blinding brightness of day, Francisco Manoel makes his way through the alleys of the completely deserted city. Not a single person to be seen. He is tired and sweaty. He glances into a side alley that seems to writhe from the heat and the light. No one in the courtyards, not a soul on the roofs. Francisco Manoel finds himself in a ghost town.

When he reaches the great square before the palace, he sees something utterly unreal: the square is occupied by dancers, stamping the swirling sand in a wild rhythm, but without music; no drums can be heard. The complete silence seems to drone. Then, all of a sudden, the dancers take silently to their heels.

Abomey, River

On the far side of the city, at some distance, a broad, sand-brown river flows, like a border marking the beginning of the semi-desert. Francisco Manoel stands on the flat roof of an unoccupied mud house and looks out. He sees a mighty procession of hundreds of large, black barges slowly moving away. At the front of the convoy the most splendid barge has raised a sail, like those portrayed in ancient Egyptian grave reliefs. An entire people is moving away, crossing the river, solemnly and grandly, as upon the burial of a pharaoh.

Francisco Manoel is left behind alone.

Palace, Throne Room

Francisco Manoel enters the empty throne room. There they are, the floor tiles made of skulls, the stools, the thrones. The king's throne is empty, and before the throne of the imaginary bush king stands a spittoon, and next to it the gold sandals. Next to the throne of King Kankpé the somewhat smaller stool of Francisco Manoel, the viceroy's throne. In front of it, its shaft revealing its dark inside, stands one of Francisco Manoel's boots, and next to it, placed there with care, an earthenware pot filled with seawater.

On his stool Francisco Manoel finds the leather pouch, but the passport stone is no longer inside. And lying there he also sees the staff into which a wedge was carved for him, but the wedge has been sanded away. The staff is perfectly smooth.

Desert Landscape outside Abomey

A sweeping landscape, shimmering with mirages: here the desert begins, endless, not meant for human beings. In the background, far off and looking like an apparition itself: the skyline of the city of Abomey, with the flickering battlements of the royal palace towering over it.

Francisco Manoel staggers toward us; he seems confused and

is murmuring to himself. "The slaves will sell their master and grow wings," he says.

He fixes his eye on a horizon more distant than what is visible to us. "In the east there must be a high mountain; the Mahis tell tales of it. It is so high, they say, that snow lies on its upper slopes, above the clouds. From the snow the animals acquire white pelts. The snow has a salty taste. I want to get to the snow."

As he moves away from us toward the imaginary of an entire continent, we still hear him whispering, "The snow, the snow."

Francisco Manoel stumbles out into the light, and dust, and vultures, and lightness, and nothingness.

Werner Herzog was born in Munich and grew up in a remote mountain village in Bavaria, where he never saw films, television, or telephones as a child. He made his first film in 1961 at the age of nineteen. Since then he has produced, written, and directed more than sixty films, including *Nosferatu the Vampyre* and *Grizzly Man*; published more than a dozen books of prose; and directed many operas. His books *Scenarios, Scenarios II,* and *Of Walking in Ice* have also been published by the University of Minnesota Press.

Krishna Winston is Marcus L. Taft Professor of German Language and Literature, Emerita at Wesleyan University.